BLACK DEVIL
AND IRON ANGEL

Paul A. Youngman

BLACK DEVIL AND IRON ANGEL

The Railway in Nineteenth-Century German Realism

The Catholic University of America Press
Washington, D.C.

Copyright © 2005
The Catholic University of America Press
All rights reserved

The paper used in this publication meets the minimum requirements of American National Standards for Information Science—Permanence of Paper for Printed Library Materials, ANSI Z39.48-1984.
∞

LIBRARY OF CONGRESS CATALOGING-IN-PUBLICATION DATA
Youngman, Paul A., 1965–
    Black devil and iron angel : the railway in nineteenth-century German realism / Paul A. Youngman.— 1st ed.
        p. cm.
    Includes bibliographical references.
    ISBN 13: 978-0-8132-1416-0 (cloth : alk. paper)
    ISBN 10: 0-8132-1416-5 (cloth : alk. paper)
    1. German literature—19th century—History and criticism. 2. Railroads in literature. I. Title.
PT345.Y68 2005
830.9´356—dc22

2004017342

IN MEMORIAM

Peter A. Youngman (1941–2002)

Vim, Vigor, and Vitality

CONTENTS

Preface ix
Abbreviations xiii

1. Introduction 1
History of the German Railway / 4
Purveyor of Culture or Culture Killer? / 9
Survey of Current Research / 12
Realism and the Railway / 16
Overview of the Primary Literature / 23

2. Berthold Auerbach 27
"Auf einem Acker an der Eisenbahn" / 29
Auerbach and Realism / 31
Sträflinge / 39
Das Nest an der Bahn / 45

3. Peter Rosegger 55
Rosegger, Auerbach, and Realism / 57
Essays on Progress / 60
"Der Dorfbahnhof" / 64
Die neue Bahn / 67
Das ewige Licht / 73

4. Theodor Fontane 84
Fontane's Realism / 86
Cécile / 89
Effi Briest / 100

5. **Gerhart Hauptmann** 109
Hauptmann, Realism, and Mythology / 112
"Im Nachtzug" / 115
Bahnwärter Thiel / 121

6. **Max Eyth** 128
"Poesie und Technik" / 130
"Die Brück' am Tay" / 134
Berufstragik / 138

7. **Conclusion** 149

Appendix A. "Im Nachtzug" 155
Appendix B. "Die Brück' am Tay" 159
Bibliography 163
Index 169

PREFACE

While driving to work one day in September 1996, I was listening to a story on National Public Radio comparing the cultural reception of the railway in the nineteenth century with the reception of computer networks in the twentieth century. I thought to myself, "Now there's an interesting project." I began research and was immediately struck by the troubled reception of the railway in nineteenth-century Germany. It was, as my title suggests, both a "schwarzer Teufel" ("black devil") and an "eiserner Engel" ("iron angel"). I was so struck by this dichotomy, in fact, that I abandoned computer networks and focused solely on the train.

As a Germanist specializing in the nineteenth century, I further narrowed my focus to the reception and representation of the railway by a variety of German realist authors, including Berthold Auerbach, Theodor Fontane, and Gerhart Hauptmann. The explicit mythologizing of the rail (devil, angel), led me to focus on the point at which myth and technology merge—these responses to the railway suggested a larger narrative made up of both scientific and nonscientific explanations that humans seem to need in order to achieve some sense of control over a world in which they have little power.

Using Theodor Adorno and Max Horkheimer's seminal work on the dialectic of the Enlightenment as a framework, it becomes clear that realist authors are a particularly rich source in which to study this intersection of myth and technology.

Realists often introduce scientific ideas and technological developments in order to bolster the claim that what they write is "real." Yet they cannot seem to divorce these developments from myth. They either couch the train and its associated technologies in mythological terms, or they show how it begins to create its own myths. Thus, as Adorno and Horkheimer posit, technology never really separates itself from myth, and it often develops a mythology of its own.

I am also indebted to C. P. Snow for my intellectual framework. In his famous essays, "The Two Cultures" (1959) and "The Two Cultures: A Second Look" (1963), he highlights a rift between the world of science and the world of letters. To mend this rift, he calls for the development of a third culture, that is, for study of the point at which the humanities and the sciences merge. In looking at the era when the rift began in earnest, I have found that there were "third-culturalists," namely, the realist authors included in this study, who lived and worked before Snow coined the term. I intend this book as a contribution to third-culture studies.

I would like to express my gratitude to those who helped make this project a reality. Siegfried Mews at the University of North Carolina at Chapel Hill and Peter McIsaac at Duke University provided me with critical input and timely readings. Ana-Isabel Aliaga-Buchenau, a friend and colleague at the University of North Carolina at Charlotte, with her boundless enthusiasm was a constant source of encouragement. Stephen Miller, friend, neighbor, and gadfly of sorts, pointed me in the direction of Peter Watson's work. I wish to thank Rebecca Flannagan, editor of the journal *Postscript,* for allowing me to include portions of my article "Theodor Fontane's *abermaliger* Zug: Myth, Enlightenment, and the Train in *Cécile* and *Effi Briest,*" in Chapter 4. I am also indebted to David McGonagle and his staff at the Catholic University of America Press for taking a chance on a new author. Finally, this work is dedicated to my entire family, but most especially to the memory of my father, Peter A. Youngman, whose boys live to make him proud, drawing constant inspiration from his steadfastness, smarts, and love of his family.

Paul A. Youngman
Chapel Hill, 2004

ABBREVIATIONS

AE   Berthold Auerbach, "Auf einem Acker an der Eisenbahn," in *Gesammelte Schriften* (Stuttgart: J. G. Cottasche, 1857–58), 17:214–17.

B   Max Eyth, *Berufstragik,* in *Hinter Pflug und Schraubstock: Skizzen aus dem Taschenbuch eines Ingenieurs* (Stuttgart: Deutsche Verlags Anstalt, n.d.), 415–557.

BT   Gerhart Hauptmann, *Bahnwärter Thiel,* in *Sämtliche Werke,* comp. Hans-Egon Hass (Berlin: Propyläen, 1963), 6:35–67.

C   Theodor Fontane, *Cécile,* in *Romane, Erzählungen, Gedichte,* sec. 1, vol. 2 of *Sämtliche Werke,* ed. Walter Keitel (Munich: Hanser, 1962), 141–317.

D   Peter Rosegger, "Der Dorfbahnhof," in *Alpensommer* (Leipzig: L. Staackmann, 1938), 262–69.

DNB   Berthold Auerbach, *Das Nest an der Bahn,* in *Auerbachs Sämtliche Schwarzwälder Dorfgeschichten* (Stuttgart: J. G. Cottasche, n.d.), 10:1–126.

EB   Theodor Fontane, *Effi Briest,* in *Romane, Erzählungen, Gedichte,* sec. 1, vol. 4 of *Sämtliche Werke,* ed. Walter Keitel (Munich: Hanser, 1963), 7–296.

EL   Peter Rosegger, *Das ewige Licht* (Munich: L. Staackmann, n.d.).

NB   Peter Rosegger, *Die neue Bahn* (Berlin: Deutsche Landbuchhandlung, 1924).

PT   Max Eyth, "Poesie und Technik," in *Lebendige Kräfte: Sieben Vorträge aus dem Gebiete der Technik* (Berlin: Springer, 1905), 1–24.

S   Berthold Auerbach, *Sträflinge,* in *Gesammelte Schriften* (Stuttgart: J. G. Cottasche, 1857–58), 3:1–100.

BLACK DEVIL
AND IRON ANGEL

[1]

INTRODUCTION

> *The emblem above the entrance gate of science reminds all of its mission—namely, to make existence appear comprehensible and thus justified; and if reasons do not suffice, myth has to come to their aid in the end—myth which I have just called the necessary consequence, indeed the purpose of science.*
>
> Friedrich Nietzsche, *The Birth of Tragedy* (1872)

In 1846, when Berthold Auerbach published *Sträflinge (Convicts)*, part of his popular *Schwarzwälder Dorfgeschichten (Black Forest Village Tales)*, the entire German railway system was eleven years old and consisted of a mere 3,291 kilometers. By the time Max Eyth published his technological novella *Berufstragik (Occupational Tragedy)* (1899), the system consisted of an iron net that encompassed more than fifty thousand kilometers in the German territory—a more than fifteen-fold increase.[1] Given this explosive growth rate, it is hardly surprising that the train and its associated technologies became a focus of study in German society, particularly in the realm of literature. With *Sträflinge* and *Berufstragik* serving as beginning and end points, respectively, I propose to

---

1. Rainer Fremdling, "Industrialisierung und Eisenbahn," in *Zug der Zeit—Zeit der Züge: Deutsche Eisenbahn, 1835–1985,* ed. Manfred Jehle and Franz Sonnenberger (Berlin: Siedler, 1985), 1:131.

analyze the treatment of the railway in a variety of nineteenth-century literary texts that reflect a wide spectrum of perspectives on the development and impact of the railway on German society.

Through an analysis of the fiction and nonfiction of Berthold Auerbach, Theodor Fontane, Gerhart Hauptmann, Peter Rosegger, and Max Eyth, I will demonstrate that despite the intellectual movement in Germany and Austria toward a scientific and technologically oriented worldview, toward a hegemonic scientific narrative, neither poetry nor its associated mythological narratives were in danger of being extinguished, as many thinkers of the time feared.

We need at the outset to clarify the meaning of myth or mythological narrative. Expanding on a definition proffered by Glen Guidry, I contend that myths are narratives composed of basic patterns of images, events, or situations already known to us in our cultural tradition that provide a nonscientific explanation of the natural world. Myth recurs in various formulations, literary and otherwise.[2] This work shows that these nonscientific mythological narratives and scientific, technological narratives cannot be separated and, as Theodor Adorno and Max Horkheimer hypothesize in *Dialectic of Enlightenment* (1944), that they paradoxically tend to (re)create one another.

The close relationship between myth and technology is not simply a nineteenth- or mid-twentieth-century idea. It is a conundrum that we still face today. In *The Modern Mind* (2001), Peter Watson argues that science and the arts are parts of one story humans use to attempt to understand themselves and their surroundings. He emphasizes the importance of comprehending this larger narrative and its evolution, which naturally involves an understanding of science, history, and the patterns that underlie both. At the same time, the narrative is also shaped by religion and the arts. They too have assisted humankind in its "at-

---

2. Glen A. Guidry, "Myth and Ritual in Fontane's *Effi Briest*," *Germanic Review* 59, no. 1 (1984): 19–25.

tempts to come to terms with both the natural and the supernatural world, to create beauty, produce knowledge, and get at the truth."[3]

In our emphasis on the legitimacy of both approaches to understanding, Watson and I follow the lead of Charles Percy Snow, who in the mid-twentieth century identified what he considered a dangerous rift between literary intellectuals on the one hand and scientists on the other. In order to prevent the establishment of two distinct cultures incapable of communicating with each other, he admonished intellectuals to establish a "third culture," one that would bridge the gap between the techno-scientific realm and the mytho-literary realm.[4] My project is intended as a contribution to what has become known as "third-culture studies." In an effort to make the discussion of such a broad concern more manageable, I have focused my analysis on one innovation, the train, in the context of the latter half of the nineteenth century, and on the authors of its dominant literary movement—realism—many of whom were espousing third-culture views before the term was even coined.

Realism marks the beginning of a literary coming-to-terms with an era that is increasingly interested in science and technology, the former as a means of ascertaining a stable, knowable reality, the latter as a manifestation of this reality. Realists, like scientists, proposed to ascertain and depict reality, and thus borrowed liberally from the world of science. For example, just as science is based on observation, the role of observation in the realist novel is "proportionately greater than that of artistic convention."[5] This concept of observation implies objectivity, an ascertaining of the facts, of "truth," as it were. Realists reinforced their claims to "truth" by introducing scientific and technologi-

3. Peter Watson, *The Modern Mind: An Intellectual History of the Twentieth Century* (New York: Harper-Collins, 2001), 771.

4. C. P. Snow, "The Two Cultures," in C. P. Snow, *The Two Cultures* (1959; Cambridge: Cambridge University Press, 1993), 3.

5. Lilian Furst, *All Is True: The Claims and Strategies of Realist Fiction* (Durham: Duke University Press, 1995), 6.

cal developments into their work. But this version of reality is just one version, a version that was necessarily aestheticized and therefore inseparable from the mythical. As Lilian Furst says, the divide between the real and the mythical is not clear.[6] Realist authors could no more transcend myth than could scientists or anyone else. They relate the narrative, as Watson suggests, and thus they provide a rich body of work in which to analyze the rather complicated relationship between myth and technology.

History of the German Railway

Before delving more deeply into these issues, a brief history of the railway in Germany is necessary. The impetus behind the development of the railway in Germany came from Friedrich List, its "spiritual father." List outlined his revolutionary vision in an 1841 work entitled *Kräfte und Mächte (Forces and Powers)*. In a chapter entitled "Zum nationalen Eisenbahnsystem" (Regarding a National Rail System), he not only articulated a startlingly accurate view of a future rail network, he singled out the advantages that an extensive railway system would confer on Germany.[7] Inasmuch as the railway would allow the rapid movement of troops to trouble spots, it was necessary as a *Nationalverteidigungsinstrument* (instrument of national defense). The railway would speed the exchange of scientific and artistic ideas and thus act as a *Kulturbeförderungsmittel* (purveyor of culture). As a major force toward industrialization, the railway would increase prosperity and prove itself as an *Assekuranzanstalt* (insurance agency). It would serve as a *Gesundheitsanstalt* (health agency) by more efficiently connecting the suffering with a

---

6. Ibid., 163.
7. List was an early and outspoken proponent of unification; thus his premature use of the word "nation" with regard to German-speaking lands is indicative of that which was obvious to him—that unification would come soon and would be fostered by the railway.

cure. Far-flung friends and family would see one another more frequently by using the train as a *Vermittler des gemütlichen Verkehrs* (promoter of social relations). By opening the country to more efficient travel, the railway would eliminate provincialism and prejudice and strengthen the *Nationalgeist* (national spirit). It would unify the country by serving as a *fester Gürtel um die Lenden der deutschen Nation* (secure belt around the haunches of the German nation). Finally, the railway would be the *Nervensystem des Gemeingeistes* (the nerve system of the public spirit) and thus place the people on equal footing with the state.[8] In short, a rail system in the regions that would ultimately constitute the future German nation would forge a well-defended, intellectual, wealthy, healthy, happy, prejudice-free, unified democratic state. This was a remarkably tall order for a system that at the time consisted of only 677 kilometers.[9]

Although List did not live to see, let alone direct, the development of the railway, his tall order was filled at least in part. As an instrument of military defense or offense, the railway played a well-documented, critical role in the logistics of the Schleswig-Holstein War of 1864, the Austrian War of 1866, and the Franco-Prussian War of 1870–71, and in this sense helped achieve the goal of unification. In addition, in the twentieth century Germany used the rail as a reliable, effective means of projecting its power in both world wars and to a much more pernicious end in the Holocaust of the Second World War.

There is also no doubt that the rail served as an economic engine in both centuries. Heinimann points out that the railway sparked striking growth in heavy industry; thanks to the railway, the price of transportation was significantly cut and thus the prices of other goods such as food and fuel were reduced as well.[10] Between 1850 and 1871 the rail accounted for 14 percent

---

8. Friedrich List, *Kräfte und Mächte* (1841; Munich: Langewiesche-Brandt, 1942), 179–81.
9. Fremdling, "Industrialisierung und Eisenbahn," 131.
10. Alfred Ch. Heinimann, *Technische Innovation und literarische Aneigung:*

to 20 percent of German economic investment; by 1879 the figure had increased to approximately 25 percent. The railway was an economic engine if ever there was one.[11] In terms of rail equipment alone, the increases are dramatic. In 1839 Germany produced no rail engines of its own; by 1853 it produced 94 percent of its engines. The same holds true for the rails themselves. In 1843 10 percent of the rails were German-made, while in 1863 85 percent were produced in Germany. The railway workforce increased from 26,000 workers in 1850 to 204,900 in 1866.[12] These statistics reflect an unprecedented boost in the German economy spurred by an economic engine that was on its way to becoming the largest enterprise in the capitalist world in the early twentieth century.[13]

Of the eight advantages of the railway enumerated by List, the military and economic aspects discussed above are the only ones that do not seem to be subject to debate. For example, the railway seemed, for a time, to boost the position of average citizens, to place them on equal footing with the powers that be. It was, after all, one impetus behind a shift from a feudal, absolutist, agrarian state to a liberal, bourgeois, industrial state. Early on, the nobility feared that the railway would lead to class equality. For example, King Ernst August von Hannover "[wollte] nicht, dass jeder Schuster und Schneider so rasch reisen kann wie [er]" (did not want every shoemaker and tailor to be able to travel as quickly as [he]).[14] As Mahr points out, there was a discernible feeling of independence at the time, a sense that the king was viewing something conceived, built, and run by the common

---

Die Eisenbahn in der deutschen und englischen Literatur des 19. Jahrhunderts (Bern: Francke, 1992), 39.

11. Fremdling, "Industrialisierung und Eisenbahn," 132.

12. Abigail Green, *Fatherlands: State-Building and Nationhood in Nineteenth-Century Germany* (Cambridge: Cambridge University Press, 2001), 230.

13. Alfred C. Mierzejewski, *The Most Valuable Asset of the Reich: A History of the German National Railway,* vol. 1 (Chapel Hill: University of North Carolina Press, 1999), xi.

14. Heinimann, *Technische Innovation,* 38.

man, not by a monarch or agents of his government.[15] But politicians and monarchs alike were quick to recognize the advantages of supporting the railway, or at least of appearing to do so. The same King Ernst August von Hannover who bemoaned the railway commissioned a statue of himself in front of the main train station in Hannover so that he might be known to posterity as the builder of railways.[16] Governments also began to recognize the value of the rail system as an agent of propaganda. By making state-owned newspapers available at all train stations, for example, they were assured a captive audience. Thus the potential of the railway as a source of power to the people was short-lived.

The extent of the railway's role in the unification of 1871, beyond the acknowledged military advantages it afforded, is also subject to debate. Markus Völkel argues that unification was more a result of Prussian power politics and cannot be attributed directly to the advent of rail. His evidence, simply put, is that even after unification the railways remained under the control of individual German states.[17] Thus the story of the railway, according to Völkel, is a story of particularism and not of nationalism. Abigail Green lays out a more reasonable position. She argues that "there can be no doubt that railways played a crucial role in fostering economic integration and encouraging the creation of national markets in Germany.... Ultimately, however, the impact of railway construction [on unification] in Germany remained ambivalent."[18] While Green does not dispute the particularist nature of the railway, she does grant a greater role to

15. Johannes Mahr, *Eisenbahnen in der deutschen Dichtung: Der Wandel eines literarischen Motivs im 19. und im beginnenden 20. Jahrhundert* (Munich: Fink, 1982), 41.
16. Green, *Fatherlands,* 259.
17. Markus Völkel, "Einigkeit und Freiheit: Die Eisenbahn, ein Mittel nationaler Politik," in Jehle and Sonnenberger, *Zug der Zeit—Zeit der Züge,* 1:224.
18. Green, *Fatherlands,* 266.

the railway in promoting unification than do Völkel and his ilk.

Even more problematic than the question of unification is List's prediction that the railway would strengthen the *Nationalgeist* (national spirit). The railway clearly did not forge a happy, intellectual nation. In addition, the idea of the train as a *Vermittler des gemütlichen Verkehrs* (promoter of social relations) was called into question by Freud in the early twentieth century. In *Civilization and Its Discontents* (1930), he wrote, "If there had been no railway to conquer distances, my child would never have left his native town and I should need no telephone to hear his voice; if traveling across the ocean by ship had not been introduced, my friend would not have embarked on his sea voyage and I should not need a cable to relieve my anxiety about him."[19] He thereby dismissed the railway and technological innovation in general as a wash.

The question of a nation free of prejudice is less problematic than the concept of the rail as a *Vermittler des gemütlichen Verkehrs* (promoter of social relations). This is most obvious with regard to the "Jewish question." In his essay "Ein Tag in der Heimat" (One Day in My Homeland), which appeared in *Deutsche Rundschau* in 1879, Berthold Auerbach hoped for the same mind-broadening impact of the rail that List did, but he understood that, just as the train could bring freedom, it could also bring "Plagen und Störungen" (plagues and disturbances). The train might hinder anti-Semitism or it might increase its spread, and Auerbach was not prepared to pass judgment in 1879.[20] Anti-Semitism was alive and well in Germany, as in Europe in general in the nineteenth century, and it culminated, but by no means disappeared, with the end of the Second World War in 1945. It would be problematic, to say the least, to credit the burgeoning rail system with either the ebb or the flow of racist sentiment.

19. Sigmund Freud, *Civilization and Its Discontents,* in *The Freud Reader,* ed. Peter Gay (New York: W. W. Norton, 1995), 736.
20. Berthold Auerbach, "Ein Tag in der Heimat," *Deutsche Rundschau* 23 (1880): 301.

Although Green makes an attempt, it is also difficult to evaluate the railway's impact on the cultural and intellectual life of Germany in terms of spreading scientific and aesthetic ideas. Green presents evidence of increased participation in the *Cannstatter Volksfest* (Canstatt Fair), which became a truly statewide festival with the advent of rail. She also cites increased attendance at the Historical Museum in Dresden, the inspector of which credited the popularity of rail travel, an inexpensive mode of transportation, for allowing more people to enjoy the museum's art collection. This, Green concludes, is proof that the railway increased the impact of state-sponsored cultural events.[21] Whether this is the scale of cultural dissemination that List envisioned or whether this truly correlates to a wider dissemination of the arts and sciences is not entirely clear.

While it may ever remain ambiguous whether the railway itself was able to spread aesthetic ideas and thus positively affect the culture, it is certain that the railway in a sense became its own aesthetic idea. Many authors of the late nineteenth and early twentieth centuries, some influential and others less so, used the railway as an integral literary device in their work. In this way alone, the rail had a tremendous impact on the world of ideas.

Purveyor of Culture or Culture Killer?

In many of the works analyzed in this book, writers weighed in on the concept of the railway as a *Kulturbeförderungsmittel* (purveyor of culture). Some saw it as an extensive root system that promised to nurture the culture in general. Others were not so enthusiastic about the newly formed iron net and saw it as a device that constricted the lifeblood of the culture. These two opposing viewpoints were indicative of the larger reception of

21. Green, *Fatherlands,* 256–58.

the railway. The metaphors employed to describe the train in the nineteenth century highlight the dichotomy. Those who considered the railway a nurturer of sorts described the train as a *Triumphwagen des Gewerbefleißes* (triumphal car of industriousness), a *Leichenwagen des Absolutismus* (funeral car of absolutism), or an *eisernen Engel* (iron angel). Those who saw it as constrictive called it a *schwarzen Teufel* (black devil), a *Feuerdrachen* (fiery dragon), or a *Saat von Drachenzähnen* (seed of dragon's teeth).[22]

Auerbach's praise of the railway in "Ein Tag in der Heimat" belongs to the first camp. "Die Eisenbahn," he wrote, "ermöglicht es, nach jedem stillen Fleck der Erde alle Bequemlichkeiten und Schönheiten der Cultur zu versetzen" (The railway made it possible to promote all of the creature comforts and beauty of the culture in every single solitary spot on earth).[23] For Auerbach, the railway could not only serve as a deliverer of the "creature comforts," it was also a potential mechanism of education and a means of transporting the "beautiful" in German culture to even the remotest regions. Consider also this entry in the 1846 edition of Meyer's *Conversations-Lexicon:* "In Bezug auf ihren [der Eisenbahn] Enfluß, auf das Wohlseyn und die Bildung der gewerblichen Klassen möchte man sie den Messias . . . nennen. Kein Zweifel, daß in der neuen Fortbewegung ein Keim allgemeiner Glückseligkeit liegt, stärker, kräftiger, mehr versprechender als alle frühern. Durch die neuen Transportmittel wird der Mensch ein unendlich höheres, vermögenderes, vollkommneres Wesen" (With regard to the influence of the railway on the well-being and education of the middle class, one may call it the Messiah. . . . There is no doubt that in this new age of movement lies the seed of general happiness, more strongly, more powerfully, and more promisingly than in all earlier eras. Through the new means of transportation, mankind will become an infinitely higher, wealthier, and more

---

22. Mahr, *Eisenbahnen in der deutschen Dichtung*, 124.
23. Auerbach, "Ein Tag in der Heimat," 289.

perfect being).[24] In sum, German society had encountered an innovation in the railway that promised to deliver education, prosperity, and power to the average citizen—to boost a nascent shift from a feudal-agrarian collection of independent states to a technologically advanced industrial nation.

Other writers were not quite prepared to equate technological advances such as the railway system with human progress. I have already noted Freud's early twentieth-century take on technology in *Civilization and Its Discontents*. Writing forty years later, Wolfgang Schivelbusch echoed this sentiment in *The Railway Journey* (1977) when he pointed to the dialectic of this process: the apparent "diminution of space (i.e., the shrinking of transport time) actually caused an expansion of transport space by incorporating new areas into the transport network. The nation's contraction into a metropolis . . . conversely appeared as an expansion of the metropolis: by establishing transport lines to ever more outlying areas, the metropolis tended to incorporate the entire nation."[25] Freud and Schivelbusch emphasized the paradox inherent in rail technology: the world becomes both smaller and larger, frightening and tame at the same time.

Heinrich Heine was one writer who saw the frightening side of the railway. In a letter written on the occasion of the opening of a new rail line in Paris, he wrote that because of the development of the railway, "erfaßt den Denker ein unheimliches Grauen, wie wir es immer empfinden, wenn das Ungeheuerste, das Unerhörteste geschieht, dessen Folgen unabsehbar und unberechenbar sind" (an uncanny horror grips the philosopher, as it always does when the monstrous and the unheard of takes place, the consequences of which are unforeseeable and in-

---

24. *Das große Conversations-Lexicon für gebildete Stände,* vol. 8 (Hildburghausen: J. Meyer, 1846), 154–55.
25. Wolfgang Schivelbusch, *The Railway Journey: The Industrialization of Time and Space in the Nineteenth Century* (Hamburg: Berg, 1977), 35.

calculable).²⁶ What is it about the human condition that causes us to simultaneously praise and damn technological innovation? As Freud put it, "with every tool man is perfecting his own organs, whether motor or sensory, or is removing the limits to their functioning."²⁷ In Freud's view humankind ultimately fears the prospect that technology will contribute to the perfection of the human condition. In other words, we fear our own desire to achieve perfection. Is this fear ultimately even necessary? Or is it, as Auerbach suggests, "daß von jener Stunde an, da ein Fußweg durch den Wald getreten wird, die Reihenfolge begonnen hat, die zur Legung der Eisenbahn führt" (that from the moment a path was trod in the forest, the sequence that led to laying the railway was put into place).²⁸ Technological advance, in other words, is inevitable, built into human nature and easily incorporated into the larger narratives humans construct in order to make sense of their existence.

Survey of Current Research

The significance of the railway and its representation in literature has already been recognized, yet not sufficiently accounted for. Although works like Gerhard Rademacher's *Technik und industrielle Arbeitswelt in der deutschen Lyrik des 19. und 20. Jahrhunderts (Technology and the Industrial Work Environment in the German Poetry of the Nineteenth and Twentieth Centuries)* (1976) and Johannes Mahr's *Eisenbahnen in der deutschen Dichtung. Der Wandel eines literarischen Motivs im 19. und im beginnenden 20. Jahrhundert (Railways in German Poetry: The Transformation of a Literary Motif in the Nineteenth and Early Twentieth Century)* (1982) address the issue of the railway in German literature, both deal

---

26. Heinrich Heine, "Letter of 5 May 1843," in *Sämtliche Werke,* ed. Volkmar Hansen (Hamburg: Hoffmann und Campe, 1990), 14:57–8.
27. Freud, *Civilization and Its Discontents,* 737.
28. Auerbach, "Ein Tag in der Heimat," 302.

almost exclusively with the lyric poetry of the late nineteenth and early twentieth centuries. Mahr in particular dismisses the prose works of that era with the claim that rail does not figure prominently enough in them to warrant investigation.[29] Contrary to what my analysis will demonstrate, Mahr even claims that "Die neuen Lebensbedingungen, das neue Weltgefühl sich kaum in der Literatur spiegelte; das Nebeneinander, Ineinander, Gegeneinander von Technik und Natur, von Mensch und Maschine . . . wurde nicht thematisiert" (the new living conditions and the new *Weltgefühl* [fostered by the railway] were hardly mirrored in the literature [of the time]; the relationships between man and nature or man and machine . . . were never a theme).[30] Alfred Ch. Heinimann's *Technische Innovation und literarische Aneignung: Die Eisenbahn in der deutschen und englischen Literatur des 19. Jahrhunderts (Technical Innovation and Literary Appropriation: The Railway in German and British Literature of the Nineteenth Century)* (1992) proposes to fill the void left by this lack of analysis of prose works. In a massive comparative tome, he analyzes the phenomenon of the railway through both the poetry and the prose works of the age. Owing to the sheer quantity of texts he considers, however, his literary analysis is insufficient and misses aspects.

By contrast, my project offers a closer textual analysis that I hope will yield a more nuanced understanding of the issues surrounding technology and literature. Heinimann analyzes so many works (more than 150 in a 438-page book) that he cannot possibly do justice to the railway as a literary device, especially in the major novels in which this technology plays a role. I also disagree with many of his and Mahr's interpretations of these works. Mahr's astonishing claim that the railway doesn't figure prominently enough in these works to warrant investigation suggests our deep difference in view. The claim that the themes

---

29. It should be pointed out that the railway is not the only technology Rademacher analyzes.

30. Mahr, *Eisenbahnen in der deutschen Dichtung,* 124.

of "nature versus technology" or "man versus machine" are not a primary concern of late nineteenth-century literature is simply inaccurate.

Similarly, Heinimann often misreads the texts he chooses for analysis. For example, he sees Auerbach's *Das Nest an der Bahn (The Nest on the Railway)* (1876) as similar to novels of the later naturalist movement. He also claims that this work, in which prosperity is the operative word, does not show the harmony of the earlier village tales but disillusionment.[31] Nothing could be further from the truth in this work of reconciliation and social advancement. Given the scope of Heinimann's work, an occasional misreading might be forgiven, but such misreadings are unfortunately all too common in his work.

An additional concern is that Mahr and Rademacher see a relatively simplistic linear progression in the representation of the railway in literature. The more the public got used to the railway, they suggest, the less it figured in the literature of the era. Rademacher attempts to prove this point by constructing four categories of author, each representing an author's level of acceptance of the railway. The first category includes authors in the early to mid-nineteenth century who express fear of the train as an instigator of spiritual and societal chaos. Later in the century, a second category of authors convey guarded optimism and regard the train as a promoter of economic and social progress. A third group, toward the end of the century, view the train as a guarantor of political unity and social integration. The final group of authors, at the end of the century, fully accept the railway, and it figures in their work as a given part of everyday life.[32]

The problem with this schema is threefold. First, although it is possible that popular opinion may have followed this progression, authors of nineteenth-century German fiction did not. It

---

31. Heinimann, *Technische Innovation*, 233.

32. Gerhard Rademacher, *Technik und industrielle Arbeitswelt Arbeitswelt in der deutschen Lyrik des 19. und 20. Jahrhunderts: Versuch einer Bestandaufnahme* (Frankfurt: Peter Lang, 1976), 31–37.

would be more accurate to say that literary representations of the railway became more complicated and more nuanced over time, that they underwent a kind of layering in which earlier perceptions of the railway were overlaid by later ones. Schivelbusch makes a similar point when he says that all airplane travelers, regardless of how often they fly, "re-remember" fear upon takeoff and landing.[33] The second problem with Rademacher's model is that his linear progression is not very useful in addressing the perceived chasm between the realm of science and technology and the realm of literature. Rademacher's model suggests that literary representations of the train progress to the point of eventual uncritical acceptance, but this was not the case, not even by the time Eyth was writing, in 1899. Finally, while the train is sometimes depicted as merely part of the landscape, it is almost always used in addition, at least indirectly, as a metaphor or symbol in the ongoing debate on the nature of technology and its reception, as exemplified by Heine's fear, on the one hand, and Auerbach's praise, on the other.

Heinimann, for example, argues that the railway had achieved complete and uncritical acceptance by the 1880s. By this time, he writes, the train had been fully assimilated into literature, just as Rademacher argues with his fourth category.[34] Heinimann quotes a Fontane poem, "Meine Gräber" (My Graves) (1889), in which the train is mentioned only in passing, and concludes that a level of "Selbstverständlichkeit" (self-evidence) has been reached in literature. He contrasts "Meine Gräber" with Fontane's earlier ballad, "Die Brück' am Tay" (The Bridge over the Tay) (1880) in which Fontane depicts the relationship between man, technology, and nature as much more problematic.[35]

Heinimann trivializes the importance of the railway as a literary device in the later nineteenth century, but the fact is, as I

33. Schivelbusch, *Railway Journey*, 161.
34. Heinimann, *Technische Innovation*, 19.
35. Ibid.

shall demonstrate, that *all* depictions of the railway in nineteenth-century German literature comment on the relationship between man, technology, and nature. To say that the train is simply a neutral part of the landscape is like saying that the ghost in Fontane's *Effi Briest,* is (as one early Fontane critic argued), a piece of bric-a-brac left over from poetic realism.[36] Both conclusions diminish the importance of these devices.

Realism and the Railway

Another way in which my approach is different from that of other critics is that I look at the railway specifically in the context of realism, a literary movement that by its very nature could not resist the depiction of scientific and technological advances. Surprisingly enough, I have encountered no secondary sources that deal exclusively with the railway as an aspect of nineteenth-century German realist literature. Through a careful analysis of several works, I will consider the dissonance in the reception of the railway and how it is mirrored in the dissonance that exists within realism itself. The realist's conundrum was framed in an interesting fashion by a Cologne grain merchant, railway advocate, and later a highly placed elected official by the name of Ludwig Camphausen. In an 1833 speech praising the entrepreneurial boon that the railway represented, Camphausen unintentionally went to the heart of the matter:

Wir finden uns in der Zeit des Übergangs zu einem neuen Abschnitte. Keine religiöse, keine politische Lehre wird an die Spitze des neuen Zeitalters treten, und wenn man überhaupt wagen darf, anzudeuten, wem bestimmt seyn mag, die leere Stelle einzunehmen, so wäre es das Streben aller Völker nach materiellem Wohl.... Zu den wirksamsten Hebeln für die Beförderung materieller Wohlfahrt gehört die Er-

---

36. J. P. Stern, "*Effi Briest, Madame Bovary, Anna Karenina,*" *Modern Language Review* 52 (1957): 374.

leichterung der Verbindungsmittel zwischen Ländern und Völkern, und eines derselben war nämlich: die Eisenbahnen.

We find ourselves in a time of transition to a new phase. No religious, no political lesson will step to the fore in this new era, and if one may dare to predict what will fill the void, it will be the striving of all people after material well-being. . . . Among the most effective levers for the conveyance of this material well-being is the facilitation of the connections between countries and peoples, that is, namely, the railways.[37]

Camphausen suggests that the narrative that has transcended German culture for centuries is about to be subverted. For better or worse, German civilization, like most of Western civilization, had lived inside a narrative defined by religion and politics, or myth and the application of power by the state. This was a centuries-long tradition that many believed was on the brink of being replaced or destroyed. Technology was about to supersede mythology in German culture, and the railway was one component of this shift. This notion held sway among supporters of technology like Camphausen and also among technology's detractors.[38]

Wilhelm Bölsche, the naturalist theorist and one of the editors of the Berlin naturalist journal *Freie Bühne,* was one of Camphausen's intellectual heirs. Writing fifty years later, he expanded on Camphausen's ideas in *Die naturwissenschaftlichen Grundlagen der Poesie (The Scientific Bases of Poetry)* (1887). Bölsche believed that science was reality and should serve as the basis for all modern thought. According to Bölsche, human self-conceptions based on anything but empirical evidence had to be rooted out. Religion, owing to its dogmatic, one-sided approach, was the first relic to go. Indeed, religious myths had already been toppled by science. Religion, if it was to survive in some form, must become rational, Bölsche argued—not quite

37. Quoted in Mathieu Schwann, *Ludwig Camphausen* (Essen, 1915), 288.
38. See discussion of Rudolph Eucken below.

the actual replacement predicted by Camphausen, but a drastic change nonetheless.[39]

And not only religion but also literature must bend itself to the demands of the new age of science and industrialism. Writers who clung to outmoded practices and beliefs risked becoming "durchaus lächerlich und verächtlich" (thoroughly ridiculous and despised).[40] In short, writers of fiction needed to become more like scientists, basing their depiction of life on empirical research. The old mythological narrative was obsolete, Bölsche wrote. And the most effective "lever," to use Camphausen's term, in place in the nineteenth century for the destruction of the obsolete, according to Bölsche, was science. According to Camphausen, the lever was the offspring of science and industrialization, exemplified by one of its most conspicuous products—the railroad.

Bölsche's equation of authors with natural scientists has led Lilian Furst to call realism a "prodigious cover-up," "a repudiation of the essential artificiality of art."[41] At bottom, Furst argues, realist authors are not scientists but artists who have difficulty separating reality from myth because there is no clear dividing line.[42] I would take this point one step further and add that Camphausen and Bölsche's error was to assert a division between mythical narrative and scientific narrative in the first place. This division is not only unclear, it is an artificial construct. In other words, there is no way to separate religion from political power, from economic prosperity, or even from science. In fact, as Eric Downing points out, these two worlds, the mythological and the scientific, are not necessarily even contradictory; a certain "characteristic mix of reality and fiction" is always the mark of realism.[43] Camphausen and Bölsche failed to see this altogether.

39. Wilhelm Bölsche, *Die naturwissenschaftlichen Grundlagen der Poesie* (1887; Tübingen: Max Niemeyer, 1976), 4–5.
40. Ibid., 5.   41. Furst, *All Is True*, 10.
42. Ibid., 163.
43. Eric Downing, *Double Exposures: Repetition and Realism in Nineteenth-Century German Fiction* (Stanford: Stanford University Press, 2000), 195.

Camphausen was right, however, on one count. Inasmuch as the railway was used to project military might in every war from 1864 to the Second World War, it did in fact become a "lever" for applying political power. But politics is not the focus of this work. It is the nineteenth-century anxiety that technology was entirely separate from, and even the enemy and destroyer of, myth upon which I wish to focus. Mid-nineteenth-century tracts positively overflow with warnings and laments about the detrimental impact of technology on human life and culture. A good example is an 1897 essay by Rudolf Eucken that argues that man has paid for technological progress with his soul.[44] This type of rhetoric is quite dramatic and, I maintain, overstated.

In the realist literature of the nineteenth century, one finds a quite different perspective. Writers who considered themselves pro-technology naturally used established literary conventions in their depiction of the railway—there could be no disenchanted depiction of this technology in their work. This is true of the realists as well; rail was just one new complexity that forced realist authors to reread the old mythological narratives. They revised and expanded biblical and classical myths to accommodate the new. Mythical narrative has always been an attempt to explain life and thereby control it through the power of images and words. "If everywhere in nature there are Beings around us of a kind that we know in our own society, then we can breathe freely, can feel at home in the uncanny and can deal by psychical means with our senseless anxiety," Freud wrote of religion in *The Future of an Illusion* (1927).[45] Both religion and science possess this power to allay fears—this is the point at which they meet—and this is what philosophers like Bölsche overlooked. Science and religion offer the same explanatory role, and both

44. Rudolf Eucken, "Der innere Mensch am Ausgang des 19. Jahrhunderts," *Deutsche Rundschau* 92 (1897): 33.

45. Sigmund Freud, *The Future of an Illusion,* in *The Freud Reader,* ed. Peter Gay (New York: W. W. Norton, 1995), 694.

have their one-sided, dogmatic aspect.[46] Freud believed that if people were to eradicate that childish, neurotic illusion known as religion, they would need a replacement system with all of the psychological characteristics of religion—"the same sanctity, rigidity, and intolerance, the same prohibition of thought—for its own defense." In the nineteenth century science played this role, and became its own religion. Bölsche to the contrary, realist authors simply could not help but depict the relationship between myth and technology, or myth and Enlightenment.

Adorno and Horkheimer, in *Dialectic of Enlightenment,* provide the most useful framework in which to analyze the problematic relationship between myth and the Enlightenment. They define the Enlightenment as a historical program whose goal was the disenchantment of the world, the dissolution of myths, and the substitution of knowledge for fancy. Knowledge, the essence of which is technology, was the tool for this program.[47] Adorno and Horkheimer show that this program of disenchantment cannot succeed. In the Enlightenment, "Factuality wins the day; cognition is restricted to its repetition; and thought becomes mere tautology. The more the machinery of thought subjects existence to itself, the more blind its resignation in reproducing existence. Hence enlightenment returns to mythology, which it never really knew how to elude. For in its figures, mythology had the essence of the *status quo:* cycle, fate, and domination of the world reflected as the truth and deprived of hope."[48] That essence of the status quo, according to Adorno and Horkheimer, is also exactly what the Enlightenment was aiming for. The accommodation of new scientific developments and their offspring, technological innovations, in myth or as myth, is inevitable. In fact, technological innovation, a logical outcome of the Enlightenment, creates its own type of mythical

46. Bölsche, *Grundlagen der Poesie,* 4.
47. Theodor Adorno and Max Horkheimer, *Dialectic of Enlightenment* (1944; New York: Continuum, 1989), 3–4.
48. Ibid., 27.

narrative. The narrator of Auerbach's *Das Nest an der Bahn* (1876) makes this point when he asks, "Wer an der Eisenbahn angestellt ist, wie kann der abergläubisch sein?" (He who is employed by the railway, how can he be superstitious?).[49] The railway will destroy superstition, an aspect of mythological narrative, but it will create its own superstition in turn. As Schivelbusch put it, "The sinister aspect of the machinery that first was so evident and frightening gradually disappeared, and with this disappearance, fear waned and was replaced by a feeling of security based on familiarity."[50] It seems that in many German realist works of the nineteenth century, the process of habituation identified by Schivelbusch was helped along by the repetitive juxtaposition of railway technology and mythical narrative.

Camphausen's concept of religion can be equated with Adorno and Horkheimer's concept of myth. Inasmuch as the train is the symbol or lever of material well-being, it displaces the power previously vested in religion. Camphausen, as a representative of the enlightened world, attempts to "objectify the spirit," to use Adorno's phrase, and in so doing he proposes that the object, the train, can be de-spiritualized, or, in Adorno and Horkeimer's words, disenchanted.[51] One can look at the settlement of this power dispute in one of three ways. Either mythology wins out over enlightenment, or enlightenment wins out over mythology, or—most likely—enlightenment can never really separate itself from myth, and in its attempt to disenchant creates its own myth through the same process of repetition that is characteristic of myth. Bölsche, like Camphausen, misses the intertwined nature of myth and enlightenment, or religion and science. He could not see that science was becoming the new religion of the nineteenth century. Auerbach prefigures the Adorno-Horkheimer position in "Ein Tag in der Heimat,"

---

49. Berthold Auerbach, "Das Nest an der Bahn," in *Auerbachs Sämtliche Schwarzwälder Dorfgeschichten* (Stuttgart: J. G. Cottasche, n.d. [1876]), 10:12.
50. Schivelbusch, *Railway Journey*, 161.
51. Adorno and Horkheimer, *Dialectic of Enlightenment*, 34.

when he writes that the railway, like all other technological innovations, carries the potential for its own "mythenbildenden Kraft" (myth-making force).[52] Adorno and Horkheimer see it the same way, only for them it is not a question of potential but of inevitability.

Dolf Sternberger's essay on life in the nineteenth century is also helpful in developing the relationship between myth and technology. He emphasizes the interrelatedness of nature and technology in the same way that Adorno and Horkheimer see myth and technology as intertwined. In the first chapter of *Panorama of the Nineteenth Century* (1938), "Natural—Artificial," Sternberger writes:

> Not only was the railroad "epoch-making" . . . it was also, if the expression be permitted, "nature-making." Wherever a mountain and a tunnel, a gully and a viaduct . . . enter a peculiar and intimate union, we find the focal points of this historical countryside, its sublime vistas, which . . . drew all contemporary attention and were viewed, copied, and flaunted in myriad peep shows. In all bizarreness, they testify that the victory of technological civilization did not plunge nature into namelessness and amorphousness, that it is not the pure construction of a bridge or a tunnel that elicits curiosity, admiration, and pride and remains above all a feature of the landscape, but rather that the construction was instantly joined by a river or a mountain, which came not as the vanquished to their conqueror, but as a friendly power asserting its prestige in this new proximity.[53]

Sternberger too recognizes a transfiguration of sorts that occurs in the landscape itself. The relationship between the railway and nature is similar to the relationship between the railway and poetry posited by authors like Auerbach. The train merely transfigures the picture. Sternberger writes, "Thus civilization did not, as claimed by its most recent and aestheticizing enemies, expel and extinguish the 'images' of nature; rather, the works of civi-

---

52. Auerbach, "Ein Tag in der Heimat," 302.
53. Dolf Sternberger, *Panorama of the Nineteenth Century* (1938; New York: Urizen, 1977) 28.

lization . . . intensely entrusted themselves to the bosom of nature, and the landscape of the nineteenth century shows the traces of such allegorical 'copulation' in its specific vistas."[54] Although the copulation analogy may be a bit strong, the same phenomenon occurs in literature. While the actual physical manifestation of the train resides in nature, its artistic manifestation resides in the mythical narratives of the past, and thus its own myth is created through repetition. The train does not and cannot destroy myth. As humans encounter more and more of the world and its complexities, they revise and expand their meanings to accommodate or transfigure the "new," which is always the source of the fear inherent in both myth and enlightenment. Moreover, the "new," as in Adorno and Horkheimer's dialectic, always re-creates the "old."

Overview of the Primary Literature

There are literally hundreds of mid-nineteenth-century works of German realist literature in which the railway figures as the "primary lever." In some works, like Peter Rosegger's *Das ewige Licht (Eternal Light)* (1897), the train is a threatening, intimidating instrument of a dark, foreboding future, an artificial innovation that destroys the happy status quo of man's harmonious coexistence with nature. In others, like Auerbach's *Das Nest an der Bahn* (1876) and *Sträflinge* (1846), and, oddly enough, Peter Rosegger's earlier novella *Die neue Bahn (The New Railway)* (1873), the train links past and present; it is a harbinger of a progressive, unifying future. There are still other works, such as Theodor Fontane's *Cécile* (1887) and *Effi Briest* (1895), that seem to demonstrate the level of comfort asserted by Schivelbusch and do not depict the train on either end of the continuum established by Rademacher. That is, the train is neither the instiga-

54. Ibid., 43.

tor of spiritual and societal chaos nor simply a neutral and accepted part of everyday life. Finally, there are enigmatic works like Hauptmann's *Bahnwärter Thiel (The Linesman Thiel)* (1888) and his poem "Im Nachtzug" (In the Night Train) (1888) that do not seem to fit anywhere on Rademacher's continuum.

I have chosen Auerbach, Rosegger, Fontane, Hauptmann, and Eyth because, on the surface, the majority of their works appear to fit neatly within the scheme proposed by Rademacher, but in their realism they also subvert it. Additionally, I have chosen Auerbach, Fontane, and Hauptmann based on their status as influential canonical authors.[55] While they have all depicted the railway in universally acknowledged works of literature, the purpose the railway serves in their works has not always been recognized by their critics. The import of Eyth's literary contributions may be subject to debate, but I have included him because, as an engineer, he lends technical expertise and therefore a unique perspective on the depiction of the railway in literature. Finally, I have chosen Peter Rosegger because of his interesting change of heart regarding the railway, which is reflected in his literary works. In terms of structure and methodology, I address each of these authors in a separate chapter, examining their various works and also, when appropriate, comparing them to works by other authors.

In Chapter 2, I introduce Berthold Auerbach as a transitional author on the way to realism. I analyze his most emphatic statement on his aesthetic theory, "Ein Tag in der Heimat" (1879), and then look at several of his fictional works, including a short narrative entitled "Auf einem Acker an der Eisenbahn" (On a Field Next to the Railway) (1845) and two novels from his *Schwarzwälder Dorfgeschichten*—*Sträflinge* and *Das Nest an der Bahn*. These last two works illustrate his enthusiasm for the bur-

---

55. While this point may be debatable today, there is no doubt that during his lifetime Auerbach was one of the most influential writers in Germany.

geoning railway technology, as well as his development as a realist author.

In Chapter 3, I look at the works of Peter Rosegger and make the case for him as a realist author. The works in this chapter include three essays that appeared in his journal *Heimgarten*—"Das Dampfroß mein Pegasus" (The Steam Horse My Pegasus) (1896), "Religiöse Bedeutung der Wissenschaft" (The Religious Meaning of Science) (1895), and "Die neue Hochschwabbahn" (The New Rail of the *Hochschwaben*) (1894). Fictional works include a short narrative entitled "Der Dorfbahnhof" (The Village Train Station) (1868), a novella entitled *Die neue Bahn* (1873), and his most significant work, the novel *Das ewige Licht* (1895). In this chapter I also analyze why Rosegger seems to have undergone such an extreme change of heart regarding technology between 1873 and 1895. While the first two works of fiction demonstrate great enthusiasm for the railway, *Das ewige Licht* portrays it as a nothing short of an abomination.

Chapter 4 covers Theodor Fontane. I analyze some of his theoretical writings, including his programmatic essay "Unsere lyrische und epische Poesie seit 1848" (Our Lyric and Epic Poetry since 1848) (1853) and a theater review of Paul Lindau's *Der Zug nach dem Westen (The Train West)* (1886) in which Fontane further clarifies his realist aesthetic. The works of fiction examined in this chapter include two novels, *Cécile* (1887) and *Effi Briest* (1895). Fontane is usually dismissed in most of the secondary literature on the railway as an author for whom the railway is merely a part of the scenery. This is an astounding claim given the prominence of the train in *Cécile* and *Effi Briest* and given how it figures so neatly in Fontane's theory of realism.

In the fifth chapter I deal with Gerhart Hauptmann, analyzing his poem "Im Nachtzug" (In the Night Train) (1888) and his best-known prose work, *Bahnwärter Thiel* (1888). In addition to arguing that these are not necessarily works of naturalism but rather of realism (or, as Holub calls it, "super realism"),[56] I also propose an interpretation of *Bahnwärter Thiel* that runs counter to Mahr's view that the train is a cause of Thiel's unraveling rather than a reflection of it.[57]

Chapter 6 includes an analysis of the work of Max Eyth, the only engineer in the group. I begin with a look at one of his theoretical works, "Poesie und Technik" (Poetry and Technology) from his collection of lectures entitled *Lebendige Kräfte (Living Forces)* (1905). In terms of works of fiction, I return to Fontane in this chapter and analyze his ballad "Die Brück' am Tay" (1880) and then move to Eyth's technical novella *Berufstragik* (1899), as both deal with the same subject matter—the 1879 collapse of a three-kilometer-long railway bridge over the Firth of Tay in Scotland. This novella is also of interest because many critics consider it Eyth's attempt to follow Bölsche's admonishment to demythologize literature, a conclusion that could be reached only on the most superficial of readings.

In my concluding chapter, I show that despite the different approaches taken by the authors in my study, all of these works have several aspects in common when it comes to dealing with the railway. They are not devoid of representations of myth or nature. They do in fact constitute a third culture in their synthesis of science and literature. Finally, and most important, in these authors' representations of the railway, the most conspicuous symbol of the industrial-technical age at the time, they did generate some remarkably fruitful debate on the nature of technology that still resounds today and informs our ongoing discussion of the perceived advantages and disadvantages of technological advances in the Western world.

56. Robert C. Holub, *Reflections of Realism: Paradox, Norm, and Ideology in Nineteenth-Century German Prose* (Detroit: Wayne State University Press, 1991), 203.

57. Mahr, *Eisenbahnen in der deutschen Dichtung*, 160–64.

[2]

BERTHOLD AUERBACH

Man überschaut die Hochebene des Strohgäus und dort zeigen sich jetzt neue Bahnhäuschen für die bald zu eröffende Gäubahn. Bald wird man auch die Schlangenwolken aus der Lokomotive sehen und den schrillen Pfiff hören. Welche Gebilde werden sich in den Kinderseelen gestalten, die in dieser neuen Welt träumen und erwachen? Der Pfiff der Lokomotive kann ihnen werden was uns der Posthornklang war.

You overlook the highlands of the Strohgäus *and note the new rail houses for the soon to be opened regional railway. Soon you will see the snake-like clouds from the locomotives and hear their shrill whistles. What images will form in the souls of children who dream and awaken in this new world? The locomotive's whistle can become to them what the sound of the postman's horn was to us.*

Berthold Auerbach, "Ein Tag in der Heimat" *(1879)*

Berthold Auerbach, born Moses Baruch Auerbach in the Swabian city of Nordstetten in 1812, was one of the most widely read and critically acclaimed authors in the latter half of the nineteenth century. History, however, has not been kind to Auerbach. His works are generally not considered part of the canon of German literature, and he has frequently been consigned to the rank of writers of provincial village stories, suggesting a certain lack of relevance. But Auerbach, as a transitional author whose works herald the beginning of the realist movement in German literature, is relevant in any analysis of realism and technology.

While an association with the realist movement does not in itself signify a nineteenth-century author's importance, it can have the effect of pulling him out of the ranks of the trivial. One aspect of Auerbach's work that was in no way trivial, and that added to his credentials as a budding realist, was his analysis of the relationship between art, specifically literature, and technology. One would be hard pressed to find a more enthusiastic supporter of technological progress, and in all of his works of fiction in which the train plays a role, Auerbach demonstrates a keen understanding of its economic and political ramifications in Germany. One of the central characters in *Sträflinge (Convicts),* points out in a highly charged political discussion that the train is a source of power, power that lies in the hands of common citizens (S 92–93),[1] truly a revolutionary idea in its time. In fact, the idea of new technological developments as democratizing agents still enjoys favor in the twenty-first century.

Just as it would be difficult to find an author as interested in technology as Auerbach, one would be equally hard pressed to find a nineteenth-century author with a more nuanced understanding of the complex relationship between art and technology. In order to explain this relationship, Auerbach uses a science metaphor based on Hermann von Helmholtz's newly discovered physical law. Auerbach suggests in "Ein Tag in der Heimat" that the law of the conservation of energy, which holds that energy can change into other forms but is never destroyed, applies equally "im Reiche der Phantasie" (in the realm of fantasy).[2]

---

1. All *Sträflinge* excerpts are from *Gesammelte Schriften* (Stuttgart: J. G. Cottasche, 1857–58), 3:1–100.

2. Auerbach, "Ein Tag in der Heimat," 302.

The realm of fantasy, or of myth, was changing, largely owing to technological innovation. These changes would not destroy mythical narratives and thus should not be feared; at the same time, the changes could not be overlooked. In fact, Auerbach believed, technological innovations could actually expand the mythical narrative, as the narrator in *Das Nest an der Bahn (The Nest on the Railway)* suggests when he says that no bad luck will befall anyone who lives within sight of a locomotive's steam. Auerbach's works are rich in examples that underscore his use of the railway as a device to demonstrate his third-culture take on the relationship between technology and myth.

"Auf einem Acker an der Eisenbahn"

Auerbach made his view of the railway in Germany very clear early on, in "Auf einem Acker an der Eisenbahn" (On a Field Next to the Railway) (1845). This short piece provides a concise summary of his opinions regarding the railway as told through the protagonist, an enlightened and portly farmer.[3] The farmer is taking a family member on a tour of his land holdings when he comes to a portion of his field that runs along a relatively new railway. He takes the opportunity to criticize the initial outcry and superstition with which his neighbors met the construction of the rail (AE 214). These unenlightened neighbors thought "der Teufel allein habe den Bau zu Stande gebracht und er fahre dahin und käme über's Jahr wieder, um seine Opfer zu holen; der jüngste Tag sei vor der Tür" (the devil himself built the railway, and he will come again next year to claim his victims; the day of judgment is at hand, AE 215). Here, to use Heine's description, the rail is presented as an incarnation of the monstrous and the unheard of. The farmer goes on: many of his

---

3. All "Auf einem Acker an der Eisenbahn" excerpts are from *Gesammelte Schriften* (Stuttgart: J. G. Cottasche, 1857–58), 17:214–17.

neighbors predicted that his field would never produce, that the trees would die, that the villages would burn. In his *Dorfgeschichten (Village Tales)*, Auerbach treats this kind of superstition in a more complicated, subtle way, but here he is blunt: superstition is plainly regressive and backward.

After presenting the villagers' view of the railroad in the spirit of the *Feuerdrachen* (fiery dragon), *schwarzer Teufel* (black devil), and *Saat von Drachenzähnen* (seed of dragon's teeth), the rest of "Auf einem Acker an der Eisenbahn" is dedicated to the positive, to the *eisernen Engel* (iron angel), the *Leichenwagen des Absolutismus* (funeral car of absolutism). The neighbors' predictions about the farmer's field are shown to be nothing but superstition: previously one of his least productive, this field is now one of his best. And why? Because the rail line has blocked water runoff and made the field less swampy. Thus, á la Sternberger in *Panorama,* the railway not only marks a technological advance but has become a part of the landscape.

The draining of the farmer's field is an unforeseen benefit of the railway. Among its other intended advantages are that "man [tagtäglich sieht], von wie vielen Dingen man noch nichts weiß, und das thut auch gut" (one sees daily many things about which one knows little, and that does one good, AE 215)—here the railway serves as the *Kulturbeförderungsmittel* (purveyor of culture) envisioned by List. The farmer goes on to praise related technologies, such as the telegraph system, that have accompanied the rail. In earlier times people would have called these technologies miracles, but he and his friends now know that they are not.

There is no suggestion in this brief essay that Auerbach sees the relationship between technology and myth, between miracle and rail or superstition and rail. He displays here no third-culture sensibility at all. Rather, we appear to have a straightforward statement that technology has debunked superstition, even in its most Christian of forms—the belief in miracles.

In this sense, technology does indeed seem to have replaced

myth. In fact, a telegraph operator explains to the farmer that man has become so powerful, "daß er mit Sonnenstrahlen malt, mit Dampf reist und mit Blitzen spricht" (that he paints with rays of sunshine, travels with steam, and speaks with lightning, AE 216). We have learned to control the forces of nature so that they work for us. This is the essence of technology and, paradoxically, also the essence of myth—naming and identifying with words and images in an attempt to assuage our fear of the unknown and thus gain a sense of control. In "Auf einem Acker an der Eisenbahn" there is only this slight hint of the seemingly paradoxical relationship between technology and myth. There are only, as in Sternberger's essay, the copulative metaphorical images of painting with rays of sun, traveling with steam, and speaking with lightning—all of these things metaphors rather than empirical realities. It is not until the second edition of his *Dorfgeschichten* that Auerbach begins to deal with the complexities of this matter in more depth.

Auerbach and Realism

The first edition of the *Schwarzwälder Dorfgeschichten (Black Forest Village Tales)* was published in 1843, a mere eight years after the first German rail line was put in place between Nürnberg and Fürth. These two events are notable, not simply because of their temporal proximity but because both were hailed as achievements that were to help mankind move into a new era—the train for the many reasons outlined by List, and the *Dorfgeschichten* because, as Edward McInnes points out, many of the critics who lauded these works did so because Auerbach's portrayal of the peasant milieu was true to life and offered an authenticity theretofore unknown in German literature.[4] These stories thus marked the transition to realism.

4. Edward McInnes, "Auerbach's *Schwarzwälder Dorfgeschichten* and the Quest for German Realism in the 1840's," in *Perspectives on German Realist*

This is not to suggest that Auerbach falls squarely under the rubric of realism; his position in German literature is and has always been subject to debate. Programmatic realists like Julian Schmidt, editor of the realist journal *Die Grenzboten,* did not believe that the *Dorfgeschichten* fell into the tradition of the eighteenth-century idyll. He saw Auerbach's works as a sort of modern idyll not quite rising to the level of realism.[5] Because they were written before the great upheaval of 1848, Schmidt saw the *Dorfgeschichten* as outmoded tales that did not convey a universally accepted picture of reality. He felt that Auerbach's reality held up only in terms of an accurate portrayal of local color, and that it broke down when the subject turned to the general German public.[6] In Schmidt's words, there was in Auerbach's works "sowohl in dieser Art des Schaffens als auch in der Beschränkung auf einen zu engen Kreis ... eine gewisse Einseitigkeit" (a certain one-sidedness due as much to the manner in which he writes as to his restriction to a too narrow milieu).[7] Auerbach focused exclusively on the lives of the peasants in his Swabian hometown of Nordstetten and was thus simply too limited in scope to suit Julian Schmidt.

Twentieth-century criticism of Auerbach's work does not shift a great deal. In the early part of the century Gertrud Bäumer lauded Auerbach's *Dorfgeschichten* as the greatest achievement of contemporary realism, but with qualifications.[8] She

---

Writing: Eight Essays, ed. Mark G. Ward (Lewiston, N.Y.: Mellen, 1995), 99–100.

5. Luc Hermann, "Die Nachwirkung der Idyllentradition bei der Rezeption der Dorfgeschichte im programmatischen Realismus," *Etudes Germaniques* 42 (1987): 18.

6. Clifford Albrecht Bernd, *German Poetic Realism* (Boston: Twayne, 1981), 23.

7. Julian Schmidt, "Die Verwirrung der Romantik und die Dorfgeschichte Auerbachs," *Theorie des bürgerlichen Realismus,* ed. Gerhard Plumpe (1860; Stuttgart: Philip Reclam, 1985), 110.

8. Gertrud Bäumer, "Dichtung und Maschinenzeitalter," *Die Frau* 14 (1907): 271.

called his work "das Idyll ländlicher Verhältnisse" (the idyll of the rural way of life) and lamented that this "Verkunder einer neuen sozialen Ordnung, die doch ihrem Wesen und ihrer Berechtigung nach durchaus die Entwicklung zum Industrievolk voraussetzte, daß dies[er] Apostel neuer Volksrechte die Gültigkeit [seiner] Ideale von Volkskraft und Volkstüchtigkeit an den Vertretern der alten Wirtschaftsorganisation darlegte. Er wird, um politisch fortschrittliche Ideale zu stützen, unwillkürlich wirtschaftlich konservativ" (proclaimer of a new social order, which in its essence and justification assumes a development into an industrial society, that this apostle of new citizen's rights explains the validity of his ideals of equality and industriousness in the context of representatives of an obsolete economic system. In order to support politically progressive ideals, he becomes unwittingly conservative).[9] Again we hear the concern that Auerbach's version of reality is too limited in scope, especially inasmuch as the new reality in the nineteenth century was the industrial economy. Although this may be a fair criticism with regard to some of Auerbach's stories, it cannot be universally applied. In his novels *Sträflinge* and *Das Nest an der Bahn,* Auerbach attempts to combine, admittedly without perfect success, his social progressivism with the realities of the industrial economy as represented by the railway.

Like his contemporaries, most modern critics are reluctant to place Auerbach squarely within the context of realism. Luc Hermann sees him as a forerunner to realism who had one eye fixed on the eighteenth-century idyll and one eye on the tragedy of the nineteenth century.[10] McInnes maintains that Auerbach did not address the "cataclysmic upheaval" in the peasant world and thereby undermined the relevance of his work—an expansion of the criticisms leveled by Schmidt and Bäumer.[11] Not only were the *Dorfgeschichten* limited in their

9. Ibid.
10. Hermann, "Nachwirkung der Idyllentradition," 27.
11. McInnes, "Auerbach's *Schwarzwälder Dorfgeschichten,*" 111.

scope, but Auerbach did not even do justice, within that limited scope, to the life of the Swabian peasant.

Auerbach's own view of his art may provide some clarification of these matters. While indebted to the Young Germany model of the reflection-and-idea novel, Auerbach saw himself as a forerunner of realism, if not a realist in his own right.[12] A closer look at his essay "Ein Tag in der Heimat" sheds more light on his aesthetic. The entire essay, subtitled "Sommer-Erinnerung 1879" (A Summer Memory 1879), revolves around a trip by foot and rail to his beloved homeland. At the end of the first day, which marks the end of his walking tour, he writes: "Mögen andere den historischen Roman pflegen mit weit auffassenden Geschichtsbildern, ich bleibe bei dem concreten Leben der Gegenwart und bei dem kleinen, aus dem sich doch schließlich alles große Leben zusammensetzt. Ich kehre aus dem Blick ins Weite und Historische wieder zurück ins Nahe und Gegenwärtige" (As much as others like to present the historical novel with all-encompassing historical images, I focus on the concrete present and on the "small" from which, in the end, all "great" events stem. I turn my glance from the all-encompassing and historical back to the near and the present).[13] While his use of "great" and "small" recalls Stifter's much-analyzed preface to his collection *Bunte Steine (Colored Stones)* (1852), a work not always identified as a modern work of realism, one does see realist characteristics in this passage. Auerbach's prominent focus on the here and now and the everyday, while the seemingly "great" events of the era play out in the background, is an important aspect of the realist aesthetic. This emphasis again points to Auerbach as a transitional artist and to his attempts to accommodate a new reality, the reality of the railway system, not only as part of the great eco-

12. Hans Otto Horch, "Berthold Auerbach's First Collection of *Dorfgeschichten* Appears," in *Yale Companion to Jewish Writing and Thought in German Culture, 1096–1996*, ed. Sander L. Gilman and Jack Zipes (New Haven: Yale University Press, 1997), 161.

13. Auerbach, "Ein Tag in der Heimat," 293.

nomic and social upheaval of the Industrial Revolution, but also as part of everyday life in rural Swabia.

To that end, the second part of his essay relates the reminder of his travels train station by train station. He speaks with various members of the community and notes with enthusiasm the great changes wrought by the advent of rail in the region. Unlike so many thinkers of his time, Auerbach did not fear the railway. As we have seen, he saw it as a natural progression evolving from a simple path in the woods. He ridiculed those who saw the railway as the destroyer of poetry. Indeed, he thought that the railway, like all technological innovations, came with the potential for its own "mythenbildenden Kraft" (myth-making force). He hypothesized, using an analogy that would please Bölsche, that Helmholtz's law of the conservation of energy applies in the literary world as well. That he used a scientific analogy is fitting, pointing up the relationship between science and myth as it does. With this metaphor he underscored the idea that nineteenth-century narrative structures were perfectly capable of accommodating innovations like the train. Moreover, technological advance came with its own energy or myth, exactly as Adorno and Horkheimer wrote several decades later. One could consider this Auerbach's law of the conservation of myth in that myth, like Helmholtz's energy, is indestructible.

Auerbach had no patience for "die Klage, daß diese und jene neue Einrichtung der Tod der Poesie sei," because "die Poesie lebte fort und trieb immer neue Blüthen" (the lament, that this or that new direction will be the death of poetry. The poetry lived on and always produced new blossoms).[14] The new blossoms to which Auerbach refers here are the new directions of his work, which can be considered a budding form of realism. He follows his concise analysis of the art-versus-technology debate with an informative discussion of his aesthetic:

14. Ibid., 303.

Es gibt sehr viele mit dem künstlerischen Größenwahn Behaftete, die ausrufen: gebt uns eine schöne Welt und wir werden Euch schöne Kunstwerke schaffen. Die wirkliche Welt war nie eine schöne. . . . Die wirkliche Welt kann sich nie absolut decken mit den freien Möglichkeiten der Phantasie. Denn das ist des Menschen und des Künstlers und seine Erhebung über alles bloße Natursein und dessen unbeugsame Gewalten, daß er in träumerischem Sehnen und klarer Erkenntniß die Idee des rein Schönen faßt und zu gestalten sucht, aus dem Gegenwärtigen und Wirklichen. . . . Eitel romantischer Dunst ist eine Kunst, die das Schöne nur in der Vergangenheit sieht, und nicht minder eine solche, die das Schöne und sein Verständnis nur in der Zukunft finden will. . . . Die Kunst kann die Welt nicht beherrschen, regieren und ordnen; sie strebt aber nach Weltversöhnung, in der die Einheit von Gedanken und Wirklichkeit [sic]; sie gestaltet und erlöst das Göttliche, das allen Zeiten und allen Wesen inne wohnt.

There are many enraptured by artistic megalomania who proclaim: give us a beautiful world and we will create beautiful works of art. The real world was never beautiful. . . . The real world can never be the exact equivalent of that produced by the freedoms of fantasy. The artist and man in general are so elevated above mere nature and its unbendable forces that, in dreamy longing and clear recognition, he conceives and transfigures the idea of pure beauty from the present and the real. . . . Art that sees beauty only in the past, like art that finds understanding only in the future, is a vain, romantic haze. . . . Art cannot order and rule the world; it strives for reconciliation through the unity of thoughts and reality; it forms and releases the divine that lives in all beings of all eras.[15]

That this passage seems in keeping with the spirit of programmatic realism does not mean that Auerbach is a realist, the proof of which lies in his works of fiction. Some of the ideas expressed here, however, are particularly striking. Auerbach, like the realists, believed that the world could not be depicted in terms completely divorced from empirical reality. This is a stark criticism of the Romantics, who, according to Auerbach, did not try to pull the ideal out of the real world but to impose their fantas-

15. Ibid.

tic ideal on the world and create beauty solely out of images from the past. At the same time, Auerbach does not attempt (or believe in) a pure mimetic rendition of reality. This is clear from his use of the term "transfiguration," coined, in its literary sense, by Theodor Fontane in an 1853 essay entitled "Unsere epische und lyrische Poesie seit 1848" (Our Epic and Lyric Poetry since 1848). The project of the realist author is to capture beauty in his art not through purely mimetic representation but rather by transfiguring the present reality. The concept in this passage that does belong to Auerbach is the idea of reconciliation with regard to realism, which could be considered a logical consequence of transfiguration. Ironically, eight years later, Bölsche would also use the concept of reconciliation in conjunction with "healthy realism."[16] The difference is that Bölsche's form of realism, to use Furst's words, denies its own artificiality. Both Auerbach and Bölsche, among many others, believed that the task of art was to achieve unity by reconciling science with poetry. But Bölsche's idea of the third culture was firmly grounded in what he believed to be myth-free science. Auerbach, by contrast, like the modern critics Holub, Furst, and Downing, understood that these two concepts, science as a manifestation of "reality" and as an expression of myth, contain the seeds of paradox. Realists endeavor to embrace the present, the everyday, but in order to create art they must rely on timeless constructs like myth and divinity, thus proving Adorno and Horkheimer's point that science and myth can never really be separated.

This paradox seems especially strong with regard to the idea of *Verklärung* (transfiguration), an outright Christian term used to describe the change in Jesus' appearance, after his resurrection, as witnessed by John, James, and Peter; but Auerbach's emphasis on *Versöhnung* (reconciliation) in this essay also has its biblical roots. The paradox lies in the fact that the everyday and the here and now are tempered through these mythological narra-

---

16. Bölsche, *Grundlagen der Poesie*, 11.

tives. The naturalists considered this transfiguration of reality intellectually dishonest and old-fashioned; but it may be that this is simply how realists create their art. As Theodor Fontane points out, "Der Realismus in der Kunst ist so alt als die Kunst selbst, ja, noch mehr: *er ist die Kunst*" (Realism in art is as old as art itself, yes, moreover: *it is art*).[17] To use Auerbach's terms, the artist accommodates the new reality to the narratives of the past; he does not dismiss the new reality out of hand as a destroyer of art, nor does he create his art purely out of the new reality, as Bölsche would have it. Auerbach recognizes the futility, even the impossibility, of pure mimesis; he purports to transfigure, reconcile, and create.

Despite his aesthetic musings, however, the majority of Auerbach's works do not rise to the standards that either he or the programmatic realists put forth for realist literature. The difficulty with Auerbach is that he exists on one of the blurry lines that divide literary periods. The Austrian author Peter Rosegger points out as much with his question to Auerbach's contemporaries: "Wie hätte sich denn der Übergang vom romantisch angehauchten Idealismus des philosophischen Jahrhunderts der Humanistenzeit zum Realismus unserer Tage vollziehen sollen, als durch Dichter, die mit dem eigenen Fuße noch dort, mit dem anderen schon hier standen?" (How should the transition from the romantically tinged idealism of the philosophical, humanistic century to the realism of our day have taken place, other than through writers who stood with one foot there and one foot here?).[18] The bottom line is that Auerbach is a transitional artist, and nowhere is this more evident than in his novel *Sträflinge* (1846) and its sequel *Das Nest an der Bahn* (1876). Although he wrote some of his works in the tradi-

17. Theodor Fontane, "Unsere epische und lyrische Poesie seit 1848," in *Aufsätze, Kritiken, Erinnerungen,* ed. Jürgen Kolbe, sec. 3, vol. 1 of *Sämtliche Werke,* ed. Walter Keitel (Munich: Hanser, 1969), 238.

18. Peter Rosegger, "Dem Andenken Berthold Auerbachs," *Heimgarten* 15 (1891): 277.

tion of the idyll, he was still sensitive and sensible enough in 1846 to note and give aesthetic form to the great, volatile changes at hand in German society, many of which were wrought by the advent of the railway.

Sträflinge

In the major secondary works on the railway in German literature, very little space is devoted to this short Auerbach novel. *Sträflinge* tells the story of Jakob and Magdalene, two convicts recently released from prison. Magdalene was wrongfully imprisoned, serving a sentence for a theft her stepfather, Frieder, committed. Jakob was in prison for killing a man in self-defense. They are helped in their transition by Dr. Heister, Magdalena's former employer and the founder and director of a charitable organization designed to help convicts as they try to make a new life outside prison. They both find employment as menial laborers in the village and face the predictable prejudices against them as ex-convicts. In time they learn to trust each other and eventually fall in love. Before they are to be married, Jakob and Magdalene are falsely accused of yet another theft, again committed by Frieder. Magdalene is immediately cleared of any wrongdoing. Jakob is also cleared, but not until Magdalene's stepfather, after some delay, admits in a drunken tirade that it was he who stole the money. Despite the setback and Jakob's attendant loss of faith in his fellow man, the two finally marry. Heister takes them further under his wing and secures a job for Jakob as a linesman who lives on the railway, where he, his wife, and their new son, Heister's godchild, will presumably prosper.

Heister is loosely and reluctantly assisted in his charitable work by a character known only as the Civil Servant, who also serves as Heister's foil. Whereas Heister represents the progressive, liberal spirit of pre-revolutionary Germany, the Civil Servant stands for the conservative element. He helps Heister only because he wants to teach him how misguided his altruism is, and because he believes that he can gain some political advantage from it. The Civil Servant certainly does not believe in the rehabilitation of criminals. This becomes clear in the chapter entitled "Der Armenadvokat und sein Freund" (The Advocate of the Poor and His Friend). The discussion between the two highlights the many differences between conservatives and liberals in nineteenth-century Germany, and covers some of the same aesthetic ground that Auerbach will cover thirty-three years later in "Ein Tag in der Heimat." The Civil Servant worries that true poetry has been taken over by authors who would lead society into its deepest, darkest recesses. He believes that art is killed by the realities of everyday life as it is depicted by the artists of the time, a theme Auerbach was to revisit and debunk time and again. The Civil Servant provokes Heister, himself a poet, to rejoin: "Ich sehe einen großen Fortschritt darin, daß selbst die Poesie jene falsche Idealität aufgegeben hat, welche die wirkliche Welt ignorierte oder nicht in sie einzugreifen wagt. Eine Idee muß Wirklichkeit werden können, oder sie ist eine eitle Seifenblase" (I see great progress in that even poetry has given up that false idealism that ignored or did not dare meddle in the real world. An idea must be able to become reality, or it is a vain soap bubble, S 19). Auerbach, speaking through Heister, is emphasizing the relationship between a "real world" and an "ideal world." "Ideal" notions that cannot become real are worthless, and thus the "real" must contain an aspect of the "ideal." Specifically, "real" things like technology have to contain an "ideal" like myth.

From this early chapter on, Auerbach aestheticizes this theme of the ideal and the real, but nowhere is it more effective than when he finally introduces the railway as a literary device. At this point, Heinimann writes, we finally understand that Auerbach is moving away from the literature of the past. In its place is a literature influenced by technical achievement, allowing a shift from the romantic idyll to modern realism.[19] That technology is quickly becoming the new faith of the nineteenth century is evident, but this is not made entirely clear until the last two chapters of the novel.

It is in the penultimate chapter, "Der rechte Mann" (The Right Man), that the railway is finally introduced. The Civil Servant sarcastically congratulates Heister on his election to the railway directorate. This is a significant event in terms of understanding Auerbach's feelings about the new technology. Heister, who represents all things liberal and progressive, is now in charge of a technology that promises to transform the face of society in German-speaking lands. The Civil Servant understands this and points out, in a most condescending manner, that it is Heister's goal never to allow the railway to become the property of the state. Heister serves notice that he will not allow the state to use the railway to bring its citizens to heel (S 91). The train should become a source of power not for a bureaucratic government but for the common man (S 92–93)—here, again, echoing List. This politically charged exchange is not the kind of discussion one expects from a work consigned to the rank of village tale. It also suggests that Bäumer and McInnes are wrong to say that Auerbach did not recognize the economic and political realities of his time. Auerbach understood, in part, the potential of the train not simply as politically but also as economically liberating for the common man. The liberation is part of Auerbach's reality that frames this otherwise idealized story of transgression and redemption.

Heister's "real" and "ideal" seem to be the focus of the nine paragraphs that make up the last chapter, entitled "Das Idyll an der Eisenbahn" (The Idyll on the Railway). The title itself echoes the paradox or tension inherent in realism. Here the reader is confronted with an idyll, generally associated with a poetic past, and with the railway as representing the reality of

---

19. Heinimann, *Technische Innovation*, 215.

the present. In this chapter the reader also learns the fate of Jakob and Magdalene. Jakob has become a linesman, and he and Magdalene have a nice home as well as a small field to tend in their idyllic setting by the train tracks. Auerbach's description conveys the tension between the "real" and the "ideal," as he puts it, or between enlightenment and myth:

Am Saume des Eichenwaldes, dort wo der Blick über die weite Wiesenebene hinausschweift bis jenseits zu den waldgekrönten Bergen, von denen eine Burgruine niederschaut: dort steht ein kleines Haus, dessen Gebälk noch in frischer hellbrauner Farbe glänzt; es ist mit dem Giebel dem Tale zugekehrt, das Dach ragt weit vor, drei Eichenstämme tragen den Söller mit hölzener Brüstung, drauf Nelken und Gelbveiglein blühen.

On the edge of the oak forest, where your eye moves over the wide, flat meadowland across to the tree-topped mountains from which a castle ruins looks down: there is a small house, whose beams gleam with fresh light brown paint. Its gable faces the valley, the roof projects far out, three oaken beams carry the wood-railed balcony on which carnations and violets bloom. (S 98)

The images that immediately jump out at the reader are the oaks, the castle, and the house. The oaks are a symbol of permanence and strength, as well as a symbol of Germany; they not only surround the house but provide structural support for it. The castle stands in great contrast to the house. It is a symbol of the romantic past, and as such it appropriately, in terms of Auerbach's aesthetic, stands in ruins. The house, on the other hand, is a symbol of strength and the living present, with its oak frame and blossoming flowers.

Auerbach does not let the reader forget that the house, while idealized, still serves as a linesman's house: "Das ist das Haus eines Bahnwärters, denn hier nebenan ziehen sich die Schienen in kühngeschweiften Bogen durch das Tal" (This is the house of a linesman because, next to it, the rails run through the valley in bold curves, S 98). This sentence, which begins the paragraph that follows the one quoted above, functions very well spatially.

On high, one notes the castle ruins—the mythological past. At the lowest point in the valley run the train tracks—the technological reality of the present. And firmly rooted in the dissonance created by these two images is the house, which is "zierlich errichtet" (delicately built, S 98). It represents a victory of "der uneigennützige Schönheitssinn" (the selfless sense of beauty, S 98). The house is art, and it is imitated or repeated, although not perfectly so, throughout the villages in the region. It is a prosaic linesman's house transfigured and repetitively imitated—two important aspects of realism. It is noteworthy that the mythological past has not disappeared; it is simply more difficult to gain access to, and it is a mere fragment of its former self. As Auerbach explains in "Ein Tag in der Heimat," "Eitel romantischer Dunst ist eine Kunst, die das Schöne nur in der Vergangenheit sieht. Jede Zeit ist ein Stück Ewigkeit, aber auch nur ein Stück" (Art that only sees beauty in the past . . . is a vain, romantic haze. Every era represents a fragment of eternity, but only a fragment).[20] Hence only a piece of the castle represents the idealized and mythologized past.

In the seventh paragraph the reader finally encounters the real present. Auerbach juxtaposes the first train to appear in the story with plow horses working in the field: "sehet, wie die Pferde auf dem Felde sich bäumen, ungewiß, ob sie jauchzen oder zürnen ihrem Nebenbuhler, dem schnaubenden Dampfroß" (look how the horses in the field rear up, [while you remain] uncertain whether they are prancing happily or expressing their anger at their competitor, the snorting steamhorse, S 99). The train is depicted metaphorically as a horse, but an artificial or mechanical horse, which itself causes some dissonance. Although, as Mahr points out, the horse metaphor was by far the most popular way of referring to this new technology,[21] it too is an interesting combination of myth and technology. In *Panorama*

---

20. Auerbach "Ein Tag in der Heimat," 303.
21. Mahr, *Eisenbahnen in der deutschen Dichtung*, 116.

of the Nineteenth Century, Dolf Sternberger notes with regard to this term that "one cannot help but admire the sovereign daring of an image that fuses this phenomenon of developed technology with the element of a natural living creature."²² Steam was the order of the day; it was the "real" of Heister's construct. The German word for horse in that metaphor is *Roß*—an idealized horse; it can be a knight's steed or a charger. It is another transfigured picture of reality, and from this train, unlike the horses in the field, the reader is certain to hear jubilation. As the train passes by Jakob and Magdalene's idyll, we also hear many other sounds—snorting, panting, roaring, etc.—it is the jubilation, however, that differentiates this train and leads the reader to the last sentence: "Das selig stille Glück stirbt nicht aus, es siedelt sich hart neben den unbeugsam eisernen Gleisen der neuen Zeit an" (The blessed, peaceful happiness did not die out; it settles in right next to the unbendable iron rails of the new era, S 100). This is a final emphasis on the paradox and dissonance that is realism. The ideal image of blessed happiness juxtaposed with the real iron tracks of the new era is appropriate. As Auerbach says, "Die Poesie [lebt] fort und [treibt] immer neue Blüthen" (Poetry [lives on] and always [produces] new blossoms).²³ The new era is a new blossom springing forth from the branch—in this case, from biblical narrative. Enlightenment, or technology, springs from myth and through repetition promises to become myth again. That is, Jakob and Magdalena's Christian blessing is, at the very least, related to this new technology; at most it is wholly derived from the railway. This ending, of course, emphasizes the idyllic. One sees nonetheless the seeds of a new realist aesthetic, which becomes more starkly evident in the sequel written by Auerbach thirty years later, *Das Nest an der Bahn.*

22. Sternberger, *Panorama of the Nineteenth Century,* 24.
23. Auerbach, "Ein Tag in der Heimat," 303.

Das Nest an der Bahn

In his brief critique of *Das Nest an der Bahn,* Heinimann argues that the idyll that dominates *Sträflinge* is not very evident; reality and day-to-day concerns have diminished the peaceful happiness.[24] He points out that Auerbach holds a pessimistic view of humanity and, with his analysis of the questions of milieu and heredity, is moving toward naturalism.[25] While there is some truth in this claim, it is difficult to see much naturalism in this piece, and equally difficult to detect a wholly pessimistic outlook in a work in which all but one character find happiness in the end. The penultimate chapter of *Sträflinge* is dominated by the image of the raven—often associated with death and destruction. The first chapter of *Das Nest an der Bahn,* by contrast, is marked by the appearance of swallows nesting in a stall—a symbol of fertility and hope. Even so, *Das Nest an der Bahn* is not purely idyllic, and therefore comes closer to the realist mark than its predecessor.

Das Nest an der Bahn brings the story of Jakob and Magdalene up to date, filling in the events of their lives in the thirty years that have passed since the writing of *Sträflinge*. Although their lives are far from idyllic, they have prospered greatly. Of the nine children born to Jakob and Magdalena, five—two sons and three daughters—have survived. The most difficult of their children, and the most promising, is the eldest, Emil, who begins as a village teacher and then becomes Heister's personal secretary. He finally goes off to fight in the Austrian War of 1866 and goes missing in action. Emil is a disappointment to his parents and the child who most resembles Frieder, Magdalene's criminal stepfather.[26] The second son, Albrecht, has chosen an interesting

---

24. Heinimann, *Technische Innovation,* 232.
25. Ibid., 233.
26. The "naturalist character" implied by inheritability of genetic traits is somewhat diminished by the fact that Emil, as a child, also accidentally

path with regard to the discussion of the train. He is first employed as a train engineer. With the outbreak of the Austrian War he, like Emil, does his duty, but instead of disappearing he returns home and is honored as a war hero. In the postwar period he becomes a technician and marries the granddaughter of the Civil Servant, who is firmly set against an alliance between his family and a family of ex-convicts. The Civil Servant's authority is greatly diminished, however, by his failed relationship with his own son, Albrecht's father-in-law to be.

Jakob and Magdalena's daughters are noteworthy in their marital alliances as well. Lena, the eldest, marries a missionary from a noble family, and Rikele marries the wealthiest farmer in the area. As with Albrecht's marriage, these alliances force Jakob and Magdalene to reveal the details of their sordid past, something they have kept from their children until now. They ultimately receive the blessing of all parties concerned—the government official, the farmer, and the clergyman—who represent some of the most important aspects of village life. Finally, the youngest daughter, Lisbeth, referred to as the *Nestling* (a well-chosen combination of the titles of both works), marries a linesman and lives in the house in which she grew up, thereby continuing the family connection with the railway.

With the exception of Emil, prosperity is the watchword of this novel, and it is closely related to the railway. The novel begins: "Kennt ihr's noch? Ja, das ist das Bahnwärterhäuschen von damals, wo Jakob und Magdalene nach schwerem verschuldetem und unverschuldetem Schicksal die erste gemeinsame Heimstätte gefunden" (Do you know it still? Yes, that is the linesman's house from before, where Jakob and Magdalene established their first homestead after difficult trials and tribulations, *DNB* 3). We see how closely their fate is tied to the railway, and we learn that in thirty years "da gedeiht und verwelkt

---

overhears that Jakob and Magdalene have a checkered past. This information haunts him throughout his troubled life and may explain his character flaws.

manches, eigentlich aber ist hier nur von Gedeihen die Rede" (some things prosper and some wither, but here prosperity is the word, *DNB* 3). Their prosperity is clearly linked to the train, which serves several functions in this story.

On the most concrete level, the train is a harbinger of good news. It also, as Heinimann points out, provides some structure, with what he refers to as "fahrplanmäßig[en] Einschüben" (timetable-like insertions) that interrupt the characters' lives again and again.[27] Although it is an overstatement to say that the trains in this book are "fahrplanmäßig" (timetable-like), they do have a structuring effect on the story, and their repeated appearance points this work in the direction of realism. As mentioned earlier, Downing points out how deeply the realist aesthetic is tied to the principle of repetition, which allowed realist authors to depict the world "'the way it is,' with all of its characteristic redundancies."[28] This redundancy connects realism with the way technology is received. In her work on repetition, Barbara Johnstone theorizes that "repetition can provide a reassuring sense of structure and order"[29]—just what many were looking for in the face of this frightening new innovation. Thus the train, with its schedules and timetables, aptly fosters a realist aesthetic function, as it does in *Sträflinge*.

The repetitively appearing train also generally brings good news, encompassing both the "small" and the "great," which is in keeping with Auerbach's use of the train as a symbol of the progressive future. One of the greatest events of the era was the Austro-Prussian War of 1866. The other great events are of course reported in the newspaper, the delivery of which, although it is not always marked by the departure or arrival of a train, is described with a railway metaphor: "Eine Landschaft,

---

27. Heinimann, *Technische Innovation*, 234.
28. Downing, *Double Exposures*, 3.
29. Barbara Johnstone, ed., *Repetition in Discourse: Interdisciplinary Perspectives* (Norwood, N.J.: Ablex, 1994), 10.

durch welche die Eisenschienen gestreckt werden, verwandelt sich durch Ausgrabungen und Aufböschungen und alles rings umher—die Einwohner und die Früchte des Feldes—wird in eine neue Beweglichkeit versetzt. Ähnlich ist es in einem Hause, in das zum erstenmal eine Zeitung kommt und nun täglich sich einstellt" (A landscape through which the iron rails stretch transforms itself through excavations and embankments, and everything around it—the people and the fruit of the fields—is set into a new motion. It is similar to what happens in a house into which a newspaper comes for the first time and then arrives daily, *DNB* 35–36). The railway brings physical movement, the newspaper intellectual movement. Even though the trains always run on time and the newspaper Jakob reads is out of date, both are still far removed spatially and temporally from actual world events. To further emphasize the similarity between the two innovations, the narrator points out that "im Sommer 1866 brauchte man eigentlich gar keine Zeitung. Da gingen die Militärzüge hin und her" (in the summer of 1866 one did not actually need a newspaper. The military trains were racing back and forth, *DNB* 49), "reporting" a great event, the Austro-Prussian War, the details of which are told only in terms of their reception in linesman house number 374 and the village.

This is because world events are not something on which Auerbach wishes to dwell; he prefers to remain "bei dem kleinen" (with the small) and "[im] Nahe[n] und Gegenwärtige[n]" (in the near and present).[30] These are the events that give form to the great, and it is these events that are most often announced by the arrival and departure of trains. In the summer of 1866, Albrecht returns home from the city behind the controls of a train. A train arrives as Magdalene prepares to tell Jakob of Lena's impending marriage to the missionary. A train on "golden rails" announces the arrival of the waldhorn, a significant gift from Albrecht to Jakob. A train arrives as the reader

30. Auerbach, "Ein Tag in der Heimat," 293.

learns that Rikele will marry a wealthy farmer. A train brings the ailing Albrecht from the city in which he has been working as a technician. He comes bearing the news of his impending marriage to Theodora, the granddaughter of the Civil Servant, who is now a higher official and is adamantly against an alliance between his family and Jacob's. A train also portends the confirmation of Albrecht and Theodora's marriage as well as the celebration of the Civil Servant's change of heart. All of these "small" events reflect greater events that remain in the background. The war is the most concrete but not necessarily the greatest of these. Albrecht's career choices and upward mobility reflect the much hoped for leveling impact of the Industrial Revolution, and of the train in particular, on German society. In fact, all of the marriages represent an upward social move for the children of Jakob and Magdalene.

A closer look at chapter 37 bears this out, and illustrates the structuring function that the train plays in this novel. This chapter begins with the arrival of the *Pariser Zug* (Paris train) and ends with the arrival of an *Extrazug* (special train), providing the chapter with a frame. The arrival of these trains also prevents Jakob from hearing Albrecht's story of his courtship of Theodora. The everyday occurrence is the fact that a man has fallen in love with a woman. The "great" historical event that is given form by the everyday has already been alluded to. It is in this chapter that we learn of Albrecht's involvement with a labor union and its stormy relationship with socialist agitators. This is in keeping with the relatively progressive nature of Albrecht's character and also reflects the general unrest among industrial workers caused by the low wages and poor working conditions that were commonplace in the latter half of the nineteenth century. Here again is the "great" event couched in terms of an everyday story of courtship, all of which is framed by the arrival of two trains and marked by the repeated interruptions of other trains. These serve as a distraction to Jakob but do not ultimately dissuade Albrecht from telling his tale. The regular, repeated interruptions in the narrative are certainly reassuring in the way Johnstone describes, but they also reflect the reality of modern life in the nineteenth century. In other words, the reality of industrialization does not wholly prevent the story from being told, but it complicates and interrupts it, a fact that is central to Auerbach's brand of realism.

The realist function of the train becomes clear in passages in which Auerbach juxtaposes the railway, representing the technological present, and superstition, which, to use his own metaphor, represents energy from the "Reich der Phantasie" (realm of fantasy). Two passages are particularly telling. The narrator says twice that Jakob does not believe in superstition: "Wer an der Eisenbahn angestellt ist, wie kann der abergläubisch sein?" (He who is employed by the railway, how can he be superstitious? *DNB* 12), and "Soweit der Dampf der Lokomotive streicht, gedeiht . . . kein Aberglaube" (As far as the steam of the locomotive reaches, . . . no superstition can prosper, *DNB* 25). Both of these statements are followed by an *aber* (but). The narrator, whom we have no reason to believe unreliable, informs the reader of the weakness of these assertions. Of the former he says, "*Aber* [emphasis added] das ist doch richtig, wenn man . . . alles vor sich selber auslegt und ausdenkt, daß es auch anders sein könnte, da macht man dem Unglück eine Thür auf" (*But* it really is true that everything could be different from how you interpret and imagine it, then you open up a door to misfortune, *DNB* 12). Of the latter he says, "Um seine Wahrheit zu beweisen, muß man *aber* [emphasis added] sorgen, daß sich da nicht doch ein Unvorgesehenes einnistet" (In order to prove the truth of this statement, one has *but* to ensure, that something unforeseen does not intrude, *DNB* 25). With his use of *aber* it is as if the narrator is throwing *Aberglaube* (superstition) back in the face of Jakob and the reader as well. Not only is the train incapable of destroying fantasy, it in fact feeds on the old mythical narrative. Jakob's declarations, we see, are ironic. In his strong praise for the railway, he is voicing the very myths and superstitions that he appears to be rejecting. Jakob wants very much for the new reality to destroy the old mythical narrative, which in this case is superstition, but his paradoxical statements remind the reader of the impossibility of that. The old narrative says that humans need protection from the randomness and fundamental uncertainties of life, which is full of pain, suffering, and menace. We see this in the figure of Satan in the biblical tradition. Auerbach makes it clear that technological advancement can never change this basic reality. The railway is no more a bulwark against tragedy and uncertainty than is a rabbit's foot or a crucifix.

In the reconciliation of Albrecht and Jakob, Auerbach drives home this point. Jakob represents the man in transition and Albrecht the offspring, the man of the present. Jakob has one foot in the past and one in the present: "[W]oher soll Jakob wissen, mit welchem Stoff man die Gläser an der Signallaterne so gefärbt hat, daß dasselbe Licht da rot und da grün durchscheint. Und doppelt beschämend war es, daß der Vater, der doch Postillon gewesen und Bahnwärter geworden, keine Antwort zu geben wußte, als Emil ihn fragte, wie man Pferdekraft messe" (How should Jakob know how the glass on the signal lamps is colored so that the same light shines, now red and now green. And it was doubly shameful that the father, who was a postman when they used horses and is now a linesman, could not give an answer when Emil asked him how horsepower was measured, *DNB* 15). Jakob remains more comfortable with the past; he has adjusted to change by preserving the values of the past—hard work, punctuality, and so on—but he is in no way comfortable or familiar with the technology of the present. This very much parallels Auerbach's aesthetic. Just as the railway cannot eliminate poetry, neither can Jakob, the waldhorn player, be destroyed by the industrial present. People use the symbols and images of the past—the "steamhorse," horsepower—to explain the Industrial Revolution. The fact is that both Jakob and poetry are simply in a state of transition.

The outcome of this transition is Albrecht, the man of the present. He starts out as a locomotive engineer and becomes a technician, presumably in some relation to rail technology, and also a union leader. But Albrecht understands the importance of the past as symbolized by the gift of the waldhorn he makes to his father. This romantic symbol of a bygone era arrives, ironically, by rail and is delivered to Jakob from the railway station. Tellingly, Jakob first uses the waldhorn to welcome an incoming train: "Weit drüben über den Vogesen ging die Sonne hinab und vergoldete die Schienen hier, und aus dem Bahnhäuschen tönte es wuderbar, bis der Eilzug kam" (Far over the Vogese Mountains, the sun sank and turned the rails golden, and out of the rail house [the waldhorn] sounded wondrously until the train came, *DNB* 61). The image of the train arriving on golden tracks to the romantic music of the waldhorn is in keeping with Auerbach's realist aesthetic; the present is depicted in the context of a narrative from the past that enhances rather than diminishes the power of the present.

We note this again in a later passage:

Beim ersten Frühzuge standen Jakob und Magdalene am Wegübergange; es pfiff schon von ferne ungewöhnlich, und richtig! Albrecht stand auf der Lokomotive. Der Vater war stramm und aufrecht wie die zusammengewickelte Fahne in seiner Hand, aber Magdalene hielt in der einen Hand dem Sohne das hellglänzende Waldhorn entgegen und mit der anderen Hand deutete sie auf den Vater. Als der Zug vorüber war, ging Magdalene nach dem Pfarrhause, Jakob aber gönnte sich's Tagwacht zu blasen, und erst, als die Glocke vom Dorfe läutete, hielt er an, nahm die Mütze unter den Arm und faltete die Hände zu stillem Gebete.

With the early train, Jakob and Magdalene stood at the crossing; the train whistled from a distance in a strange way; and there you have it! Albrecht stood in the locomotive. His father was standing erect like the rolled up flag in his hand. Magdalene held the shiny waldhorn up to her son and with her other hand she gestured toward his father. When the train had gone by, Magdalene went to the parish house, but Jakob was delighted to blow the day awake. Only when the church bells rang did he stop, place his cap under his arm, and fold his hands in silent prayer. (*DNB* 67)

This is an effective constellation of images. The man of the present rides the locomotive, which passes by the transitional man and his symbol of the past. The mysterious, romantic music of the waldhorn is juxtaposed with the distinctly religious images of the parish house and the praying Jakob. Rather than simply represent Albrecht riding past on a locomotive as a demonstration of a new faith, Auerbach chooses, or perhaps has no choice but, to poeticize this passage with the narratives of the past. Here again we see the law of the conservation of energy in action. The conversion of these narratives to accommodate present-day realities is simply that, a conversion. It does not represent destruction of the power these narratives hold but their reconciliation with new realities.

Das Nest an der Bahn ends in much the same way as *Sträflinge,* but there are some critical differences. Instead of the idyllic image of Jakob and Magdalene standing on the threshold of their linesman's house, the reader encounters the following: "sie näherten sich dem Bahnhäuschen Numero 374, am Überwege stand der Schwiegersohn stramm, und Jakob sagte zu seiner Frau: 'Das ist meine Ablösung'" (they neared linesman house number 374; at the crossing their son-in-law stood erect, and Jakob said to his wife: "That is my salvation," *DNB* 126). The son-in-law standing "stramm" (erect) recalls Jakob himself, who is described several times in this manner and who has finally achieved some redemption from the sins of his past. Through his hard work on the railway, Jakob is absolved of his past transgressions; that his daughter will create a new family on the railway is symbolic to Jakob of his absolution. This is the first time the reader is presented with the image of Jakob as a passenger, suggesting perhaps a more comfortable unity or reconciliation of the present with the past. This reconciliation is complicated, however, by the fact that Jakob and Magdalene have since been able to retire to Heister's estate, an idyllic getaway from the prosaic present. Nonetheless, Jakob has made his peace with both the present and the past, and all of his surviving children have found love and happiness. It is therefore difficult to conclude, as Heinimann does, that there is little trace of the idyll depicted in the last chapter of *Sträflinge*.[31] It still exists; it has accommodated new complexities, and these new complexities, as Adorno and Horkheimer would say, become their own mythical ideal.

Hence Auerbach does not bear out the schism between poetry and technology that his contemporaries anxiously predicted. He paints a picture of third-culture continuity that is very much in keeping with his aesthetic philosophy. The subversion or displacement of the centuries-old narrative that Camphausen and others foresaw has not come to pass. Yes, the "Streben aller Völker nach materiellem Wohl" (striving of all peoples after material well-being) is perhaps stronger than before, but it has not overwhelmed the creative impulse. Nor has science become the dominant narrative, as Bölsche and others predicted. Auerbach understood that human beings need at least the illusion of mastery over the natural world. They beg that illusion from both the mythical realm and the scientific realm, and, inasmuch as both worlds draw power from both naming and repetition, they are inextricably intertwined, as we shall see in the work of Peter Rosegger, to whom we now turn.

31. Heinimann, *Technische Innovation*, 233.

[3]

PETER ROSEGGER

Das Lerchenlied—es ist vorbei.
Doch hörst Du nicht des Geiers Schrei
Und schrillen Pfiff?
Ein schwarzer Drache schnaubt heran,
Und Feuer speit auf eherner Bahn
Das [sic] Lokomotive.

The Lark's song—it's over.
But don't you hear the vulture's scream
And shrill whistle?
A black dragon snorts toward you,
And fire spews forth on iron rails
The Locomotive.

Peter Rosegger, "An Tirol" ("To Tyrol") *(1884)*

The railway presented the same conflict in Austria that it did in Germany, and it is interesting that the conflict plays a central role in the works of another writer of so-called village tales and a friend of Berthold Auerbach—the Austrian author Peter Rosegger. Rosegger's attitude toward the railway and technological advancement in general can best be characterized as ambivalent. Rosegger noted in his journal that he was in favor of progress in cultures on the rise but against it in cultures on the wane. In rising cultures, he believed, technological progress would only enhance the improvement, while in dying cultures it would speed the deterioration.[1] This is vintage Rosegger. What he leaves unclear is the direction of his contemporary society—a question never entirely cleared up in his work, either fiction or nonfiction. Gerald Schöpfer notes that it is difficult to sort out Rosegger's positions on various issues because they often appear to be contradictory. When it comes to the idea of progress, Rosegger vacillates between glowing endorsement and intense skepticism, leading Schöpfer to surmise that he is an apt witness to a "dynamischen und überaus widersprüchlichen Zeit" (dynamic and thoroughly contradictory era).[2]

Rosegger was born in these rapidly changing times, six years after the founding of the Kaiser Ferdinand Nordbahn (1837), which ran from Floridsdorf, in the vicinity of Vienna, to Wagram. He was born to struggling mountain farmers in the Styrian highlands of Austria and became a chronicler of rural Austria's transition to the industrial age. By the time he began writing, the railway had been in existence in Austria for twenty-seven years. Thus, unlike Berthold Auerbach, he did not witness the birth and early development of the railway system in his country.

What he missed regarding the beginnings of the railway was very similar to what occurred in Germany. As in Germany, an extraordinarily strong personality, Franz Anton Ritter von Gerstner—Austria's equivalent of Friedrich List—seemed to be the impetus behind the development of the railway. The major difference was the slow pace of development in Austria, which,

---

1. Peter Rosegger, "Am 24. Mai," *Heimgarten* 30 (1906): 788. Rosegger occasionally offered his readers glimpses of his travels by publishing his personal journal entries in *Heimgarten*.

2. Gerald Schöpfer, "Peter Rosegger: Ein glaubwürdiger Zeuge wirtschafts- und sozialgeschichtlicher Veränderungen," in *Fremd gemacht? Der Volksschriftsteller Peter Rosegger,* ed. Uwe Baur (Vienna: Böhlau, 1988), 28.

as Kurt Frischler points out in his work on the Austrian railway, was primarily due to the Metternich government's skepticism about anything new.[3] Once Gerstner and his allies were free of the yoke of the Metternich reign, the pace of railway construction picked up rapidly. To measure industrialization and growth in rail traffic, Frischler looks at the kilos of coal transported by rail: 613,000 in 1842, 1.6 million in 1852, and 6 million by 1862.[4] Thus, as in Germany, the story of the rail in Austria is a story of economic growth, but it is also a story of particularism. The Austrian railway sponsors, like many of their counterparts to the north, built the railway to benefit specific regions. It was not initially envisioned as a Europe-wide system or even, for that matter, an Austria-wide system. This may be where the authors of so-called village tales or regional literature come into play.

Rosegger, Auerbach, and Realism

Modern critics tend to see Auerbach and Rosegger as "particularist" writers. The subjects of their work are said to be generally limited to specific regions—for Auerbach, the Swabian region in Germany, and for Rosegger, the Styrian highlands of Austria. The reality, however, is quite the opposite. Just as the railway could never be truly particularist in nature, these two authors did not just appeal to the inhabitants of their respective regions. Auerbach's extraordinary popularity in the late nineteenth century has been well documented, but few realize that by 1905 Rosegger's works had appeared in twenty-two languages, including Hungarian, Russian, Czech, Japanese, and Hindi, or that he was certainly the best-known author of his time.[5] He was nominated for the Nobel Prize for literature in

---

3. Kurt Frischler, *Das grosse Österreichische Eisenbahnbuch* (Vienna: Fritz Molden, 1979), 9.
4. Ibid., 12–15.
5. James R. Dow and James P. Sandrock, "Peter Rosegger's *Erdsegen:* The

1913 and was the founding editor of a popular literary journal, *Heimgarten,* that enjoyed a broad European readership and published works by Keller, Reuter, Turgenev, Heyse, and Storm, among many others. In short, Rosegger, like Auerbach in Germany, was neither a "particularist" writer nor a "particularist" public figure but an immensely popular author.

Rosegger and Auerbach are also closely related in terms of their aesthetic. Despite Rosegger's ambivalent attitude toward scientific and technological progress, his thoughts on realism and literature in general are very similar to those of Auerbach. Rosegger himself recognized many of these similarities with the older Auerbach. Early in his career he criticized Auerbach's *Schwarzwälder Dorfgeschichten* as being too provincial and not realistic enough, arguments that, ironically, were to become the chief criticisms of Rosegger's own work. He later repudiated that critique. "Damals war ich neu," he wrote, "heute bin ich ein Nachahmer von—Auerbach" (In those days I was new, [but] today I am an imitator of—Auerbach).[6] In the same article, which describes a meeting with Auerbach in Berlin, Rosegger claimed that Auerbach declared, "ich [stehe] zu Ihnen [Rosegger]! Wir haben die gleiche Arbeit und das gleiche Ziel" (I stand by you, Rosegger! We have the same work and the same goal).[7]

Their work was to present a realistic picture of village life to the world; their goal was to highlight the commonalities between human beings, not the differences. This, according to Dean Stroud, is what Rosegger called the art of humanity.[8] Like Auerbach and Fontane, Rosegger rejected the nascent naturalist movement. "Weil [ihm] die Kunst zu gut ist, als daß [er] sie in

---

Function of Folklore in the Work of an Austrian *Heimatdichter,*" *Journal of the Folklore Institute* 19 (1976): 228.

6. Peter Rosegger, "Bei Berthold Auerbach, eine Erinnerung von P. K. Rosegger," *Heimgarten* 6 (1882): 444.

7. Ibid.

8. Dean Garrett Stroud, "Idyll as Possibility: Rosegger's Humanism," *Modern Austrian Literature* 21, no. 2 (1988): 29.

Dreck tauchen möchte, und weil [ihm] [seine] Leser zu wert sind, als daß [er] ihnen nur verächtliche Kanaillen vor Augen führen möchte, und endlich, weil [er] [sich] selber zu sehr achtet, als daß [er] [sich] zum Interpreten eines ekelhaften Gesindels machen wollte.—Auch [er] sucht die *Wahrheit* zu gestalten, aber nicht gerade dort, wo sie am häßlichsten ist" (because art is too good to be dragged through the mud, and because [he] value[s] [his] readers too much to present them with disgusting scoundrels, and finally because [he] respect[s] [himself] too much to become an interpreter of a revolting rabble.— [he], too, seek[s] to represent the *truth*, but not where it is ugliest).[9] Ironically, this essay was written in the same year that Rosegger published *Das ewige Licht (Eternal Light),* an epistolary novel depicting decay and decadence as the prevailing condition of modern Austrian society.

For the most part, however, his works of fiction avoid the naturalist trend entirely. This does not mean that he created socially irrelevant idyllic fiction, however. He was more interested in reconciliation, a concept Auerbach explored in "Ein Tag in der Heimat." Rosegger, like Auerbach, wanted to reconcile the "real" with the "ideal." He was not interested in depicting raw reality. "Wer das Leben schildert, *wie es ist,* der ist erstens ein bloßer Abschreiber, zweitens ein Hetzer, denn die rohe Wirklichkeit entzweit uns stets und immer wieder mit uns selbst und den Idealen. Wer uns aber Gestalten schafft, wie sie sein sollen und auf Grundlagen einer natürlichen Entwicklung sein könnten, *der* ist ein Schöpfer, *der* versöhnt" (He who depicts life *as it is,* is first off a mere copier, second a malicious agitator because raw reality divides us from ourselves and our ideals. He who seeks to create for us characters as they should be and, based on natural development, how they could be, *he* is a creator who reconciles).[10] Again the reader is confronted with the paradox of

9. Peter Rosegger, "Alte und neue Schönheit," *Heimgarten* 20 (1896): 442.

10. Franz Haslinger, "Ein Herold Adalbert Stifters: Roseggers fünf-

realism—its attempt to reconcile a version of reality with a mythical ideal. But, like Auerbach, Rosegger holds no truck with the aspect of realism that Furst considers a prodigious cover-up. He understands that he must embrace the everyday and the real, but in order to create realist literature he cannot separate reality from myth—the characteristic mix referred to by Downing.

Essays on Progress

Nowhere is Rosegger's third-culture sensibility clearer than in his essay "Religiöse Bedeutung der Wissenschaft" (The Religious Meaning of Science) (1895). In this work he differentiates between two types of science—one arrogant, the other, the real science, humble.[11] The former is characterized by a spirit of irreligiosity, the latter by "[dem] demütige[n] sachliche[n] Eindringen in die Schöpfung, ohne dabei einem Geschöpfe Unrecht zu thun" (the humble, scientific investigation into God's creations without doing injustice to any creatures).[12] Most important, real science recognizes that science and religion are closely related. "Wahre Wissenschaft und wahre Religion . . . sind Zwillingsschwestern, und die Trennung der einen von der anderen beweist sicherlich den Tod beider" (True science and true religion . . . are twins, and the separation of one from the other will certainly prove to be the death of both).[13] This is a clear repudiation of the view of Camphausen, Bölsche, et al. and bears out

---

zigjähriges Wirken für die Anerkennung von Stifters Gesamtwerk," *Oberösterreichische Heimatblätter* 2 (1948): 320. Quoted in Stroud, "Idyll as Possibility," 30.

11. Peter Rosegger, "Religiöse Bedeutung der Wissenschaft," *Heimgarten* 20 (1895): 148.

12. It was not uncommon for Rosegger to rail against the relatively new practice of vivisection in the name of science. This is surely a reference to this practice.

13. Rosegger, "Religiöse Bedeutung," 148.

Adorno and Horkheimer's point that scientific enlightenment can never really cut itself free of myth. Rosegger says, "Die Wissenschaft gedeiht genau in dem Verhältnis, als sie religiös ist, und die Religion blüht in genauem Verhältnis zu der Wissenschaftlichen Tiefe und Unerschütterlichkeit ihrer Grundlage" (Science prospers in exact relation to its religiosity, and religion blooms in exact relation to the scientific depth and stability of its foundations).[14] Contrary to Bölsche, science need not involve any disenchantment at all, but quite the opposite. In Rosegger's view, science, like religion, brings human beings, with all of their limitations, closer to God.[15] In fact, by revealing these limitations, science also reveals the existence of the absolute, or God, in the universe. "Hence enlightenment," in the words of Adorno and Horkheimer, "returns to mythology, which it never really knew how to elude."[16]

Two other essays by Rosegger further underscore the essential inseparability of myth and technology and emphasize the interrelatedness of nature and technology. In the first of these, "Das Dampfroß mein Pegasus" (The Steam Horse My Pegasus) (1896), one sees the characteristic mix of myth and enlightenment from the start. On the surface, the entire essay consists of unequivocal and fulsome praise of the railway as a means of poetic enhancement. Rosegger believes that nothing has done a greater service to his type of literature than the advent of the *Südbahn* (southern railway).[17] Echoing Auerbach on the accessibility of remote regions in "Ein Tag in der Heimat," Rosegger explains that, because of the railway, he can visit all of the beautiful parts of the region.[18] Rosegger in fact enjoyed the benefit of free first-class rail travel in Austria for much of his life, and he

14. Ibid.
15. Ibid., 149.
16. Adorno and Horkheimer, *Dialectic of Enlightenment*, 27.
17. Peter Rosegger, "Das Dampfroß mein Pegasus," *Heimgarten* 20 (1896): 448.
18. Ibid., 449.

was therefore able to address all the regions of Austria in his poetry.[19] Again echoing Auerbach, he points out, "Ich gehöre nicht zu solchen, die das Eisenbahnwesen für den Tod der Poesie halten. Eine Reise im bequemen Waggon ist unter Umständen unvergleichlich poetischer als eine in der Postkutsche" (I don't belong to those who consider the railway the death of poetry. A trip in a comfortable rail car is, under certain circumstances, incomparably more poetic than a trip in a horse-drawn coach).[20] Although he overstates the case here, the point is that the train is decidedly poetic. In the loneliness of the train compartment, "besucht die Frau Muse den Poeten und gibt ihm allerhand Einfälle, gute und närrische, und die vorüberziehende Welt wirft auch manchen Klumpen herein, aus dem dann irgend etwas geschmiedet wird" (the muse visits the poet and inspires in him all sorts of ideas, good and foolish, and the world, as it passes by, throws in a couple of nuggets as well, from which something can be forged together).[21] Thus the "nuggets" of reality are reconciled with the myth of the muse, and the writer creates poetry on the train.

This kind of praise is uncharacteristic of Rosegger, and he cannot help but express some irony in the end. The irony lies in the metaphor of Pegasus as train, a not entirely positive image through which Rosegger expresses his usual ambivalence toward progress. To begin with, Pegasus has a worrisome maternal origin. He is the offspring of Poseidon and Medusa, from whose blood he sprang after Perseus cut her throat. In addition, Bellerophon, Pegasus's tamer, challenged the gods and tried to ride Pegasus to heaven. Zeus caused the horse to throw Bellerophon, who survived but was fated to wander the earth unknown to all.[22] This is how Rosegger ends his flattering portrait of the rail-

19. He was given this perk by the government for the renown he brought to Austria through his writings.
20. Rosegger, "Dampfroß mein Pegasus," 449.
21. Ibid., 450.
22. Michael Grant and John Hazel, *Who's Who in Classical Mythology* (Oxford: Oxford University Press, 1993), 64–65.

way, and it is a veiled warning to poets, the "tamers" of the rail, to remember the questionable heritage of the train and not try to take it too far, lest they be thrown from the rails and forgotten. Thus Rosegger subtly complicates his vision of the railway.

The other essay, "Die neue Hochschwabbahn" (The New Rail of *Hochschwaben*) (1894), sings the praises of the first railway in the Styrian region, but again Rosegger is ambivalent. Although generally in favor of this rail line, which he describes in great detail, he says that it remains to be seen whether this new railway will bring more than it takes from the less well developed regions of Austria.[23] And, in an apparent repudiation of his earlier statements about the "twin-like" nature of myth and technology, he dismisses those who claim that one purpose of the new rail is to allow people to make a pilgrimage to the shrine of holy Mary. "Wallfahrtskirchenglocken und Dampfpfeifen nicht gut zusammenklingen" (Pilgrim's church bells and steam whistles do not resonate well together).[24]

He also believes it unnecessary to judge the railway on the basis of who supports it and who rejects it. The naysayers always outnumber the cheerleaders, but all should take heart that the changes ushered in by the railway unfold not according to man's will but according to eternal laws, in which Rosegger places more confidence that he does in man.[25] This is similar to Auerbach's claim that the railway is a natural extension of the first footpath through the forest, though Auerbach stops short of seeing a divine hand in the process. For Rosegger, God's eternal laws have allowed the railway to come into existence. Enlightenment thus ensues from myth, in this case divine law, and, as we shall see in Rosegger's fiction, returns to myth as well.

As with "Das Dampfroß mein Pegasus," Rosegger ends this

---

23. Peter Rosegger, "Die neue Hochschwabbahn," *Heimgarten* 18 (1894): 628.
24. Ibid., 629.
25. Ibid., 630.

essay on a note of warning. It is the task of spiritual and civic leaders to strike a balance between nature and civilization. The juxtaposition of nature with civilization, in this instance the train, prefigures Sternberger in the twentieth century. Whereas Rosegger writes, "Die Eisenbahn nimmt uns Natur und gibt sie uns wieder" (The railway takes nature away from us and gives it back again),[26] Sternberger writes, "not only was the railroad 'epoch-making,' it was also . . . nature-making."[27] The implication is the same—technology is simply an extension of nature. The two worlds are reconciled with each other, as are technology and myth. Thus, while the actual railway and its component parts entrust themselves to nature, we shall see in Rosegger's fiction that the artistic manifestation of the railway entrusts itself to the myths of the past and creates its own myth through repetition.

"Der Dorfbahnhof"

Like Auerbach, Rosegger wrote a short narrative fairly early in his career that appears to sum up his opinion of the railway. Unlike Auerbach, however, Rosegger begins his narrative with some insight into the relationship between this new technology and religion. The narrator, ostensibly a railway engineer, opens the narrative with a comparison between a church and a train station. He maintains that artists tend to forget the train station when they are depicting a village. This is a mistake, because the train station "macht sehr viel Lärm, mehr als jedes andere Haus im Dorfe, sogar mehr als die Kirche" (makes a great deal of noise, more than any other building in the village, even more than the church, D 262).[28] Like the church, the bells of the train

26. Ibid., 631.
27. Sternberger, *Panorama of the Nineteenth Century*, 42.
28. All "Dorfbahnhof" excerpts are from Peter Rosegger, "Der Dorfbahnhof" (1868), in *Alpensommer* (Leipzig: L. Staackmann, 1938), 262–69.

station ring a welcome and a dismissal. The telegraph operator even maintains that the bells and whistles associated with train travel make him feel like the bishop, because bells ring for the bishop whenever he comes and goes (D 262).

Although the operator states this with some humor, the characteristic mix of myth and enlightenment is nonetheless apparent, and it culminates in the superstitious saying:

> Weil mitten auf dem Feld,
> Wo das Unglück passiert,
> kein Zügenglöcklein,
> geläutet wird.
> Because in the middle of the field,
> Where misfortune occurs,
> No train bells
> Are heard to ring.
> *(D 262)*

This is exactly Auerbach's point in *Das Nest an der Bahn*. Misfortune takes place in the field because there is no train bell available to afford supernatural protection. Once again the reader is presented with a new superstition couched in the new reality. The train cannot destroy superstition. The railway, like a rabbit's foot or a crucifix, will protect people from the random menace that plagues them. To borrow a phrase from Auerbach, this is a part of the myth-making force of the train. As Adorno and Horkheimer would have it, this is an example of enlightenment, specifically technology, turning into myth.

After this relatively complex beginning, the remainder of the narrative describes the various benefits of the railway to village life and falls into a structure similar to that of Auerbach's "Auf einem Acker an der Eisenbahn." Rosegger highlights the train's ability to act as an apparent *Kulturbeförderungsmittel* (purveyor of culture): "Früher hat ihm [dem Bauer] auf dem Jahrmarkt der Guckkastenmann für zehn Kreuzer durch das Guckglas die Welt in Bildern gezeigt, jetzt fliegt ihm für denselben Preis am Wagenfenster die wirkliche Welt . . . vorüber" (In earlier times, a peep show salesman sold him [the farmer] a view of the world for ten cents at the fair. Now, for the same price, the farmer can sit at the train window and see the real world fly by, D 263). Thus the farmer can experience, through a window, far-flung cultures. The word "real," however, in this instance touches on one of the main problems with realism. The farmer is riding on this aspect of a new reality, the train, theoretically experiencing the "real" world. But there is little difference between the "reality" experienced by looking at images in the peep show and the "reality" of looking at images outside a train window—both are filtered experiences. Yet this is what realists contend—"through me, dear reader, you will experience the real world, or reality." Both the peep show and the train would, as Furst put it, repudiate the "essential artificiality of art."[29] But in fact they do not. It is simply not possible for the train to be a pure means of experiencing the real world, because viewing the world from a train window is as many steps removed from reality as is viewing a painting or reading a realist novel. One can experience other cultures by means of the train, but the experience is, at best, a filtered one.

Rosegger also lauds the train as a *Vermittler des gemütlichen Verkehrs* (promoter of social relations) and *Verteidigungsinstrument* (instrument of defense). With regard to the former, the engineer points out that young people no longer have to flirt under the watchful eyes of their elders. The train offers an alternative for the suitor—he and his paramour can leave the village and return late in the evening without bothering anyone (D 264–65). On this issue of defense, the engineer boasts, "der Bahnhof ist ja der beste Freund, Handlanger und Beschützer des Dorfes. Er ist—ich spreche von den Strecken größeren Verkehrs—Tag und Nacht wach" (the train station is the best friend, handyman, and protector of the village. It is—I speak of the stretches with heavy rail traffic—awake day and night, D 267).

There is, however, one thing the train cannot defend against when it first appears on the scene. Rosegger, like Auerbach,

---

29. Furst, *All Is True*, 10.

Die Neue Bahn

highlights the initial reaction to the train by what he ironically labels "die Weisen" (the wise elders). These leaders see the train as a manifestation of the devil, and the railway entrepreneurs as in league with Satan. They bemoan the fact that the railway destroys the old patriarchal order of things (D 267). The wise elders are eventually proved wrong and become themselves great supporters of the railway. They, too, come to understand that the rail acts as a *Nervensystem des Gemeingeistes* (nerve system of the common spirit). "Die Weisen" finally admit that the train is pulling the farmer into the modern world.

Die Neue Bahn

The struggle that the village wise men undertake in "Der Dorfbahnhof" is the subject of Rosegger's novella *Die neue Bahn (The New Railway)* (1873). Because Rosegger expresses so much optimism about the train and depicts technology as a promoter of economic and social progress, this work falls in with the generally accepted linear progression proposed by Rademacher and others. In this novella, Rosegger tells the story of the citizens of a small and presumably remote Alpine village who must deal with the advent of the railway in their valley. The conflict centers on a character known only as the Postmaster, and a young engineer named Bruno Lechner who is in charge of laying the railway in the region. The career paths of the two main characters parallel their stances on technological progress—Lechner believes in its benefits and the Postmaster sees only its costs. The Postmaster refers to the railway as "Teufelei" (devilry) that destroys "die gute alte Zeit" (the good old days) and brings misery and discontent (*NB* 37), and as a "Mißgeburt des Menschengeistes" (monstrosity of the human mind, *NB* 108) that must be destroyed.[30]

30. All *Bahn* excerpts are from Peter Rosegger, *Die neue Bahn* (1873) (Berlin: Deutsche Landbuchhandlung, 1924).

There are two fundamental problems central to the conflict—the Postmaster's land and his daughter. The Postmaster owns a parcel of land that Lechner needs in order to lay the line. He refuses to give up his land, so Lechner threatens to tunnel under it, and ultimately does so. Adding further tension to the matter is the Postmaster's daughter Seraphine, with whom Lechner, of course, falls in love. The Postmaster has promised her hand in marriage to one of his drivers, Fabian Geier, if Geier can stop the railway from being built in the valley.[31] The situation is further complicated by the fact that Seraphine considers herself beholden to Geier, who supplies her with arsenic, which she superstitiously believes maintains her beauty.

In his attempt to hinder the progress of the railway, Geier, the anti-technology purveyor of superstition, sets several town buildings on fire, which rapidly gets out of control and threatens to burn the entire village to the ground. The villagers fight a losing battle against the blaze until Lechner leads a locomotive into the village with firefighting equipment from a nearby city and finally extinguishes the fire. Lechner's heroics convince the Postmaster of the efficacy of rail, and he allows his daughter to marry Lechner. Meanwhile Geier, in another attempt to hinder the progress of the rail, tries to blow up the line while the train is on its trial run. He fails, is run over by the train, and dies what can be considered a poetically just death.

This novella is not considered a great work of literature. The characters, as Heinimann points out, are one-dimensional, and the plot is highly predictable.[32] While I agree with this assessment, what Heinimann fails to see in this piece is the complex dialectic of myth and enlightenment at work. It would be easy to read the message of this novella simply as the triumph of technology over superstition, but this would be a superficial reading. In this work Rosegger demonstrates the same complex

---

31. The name *Geier* carries with it ominous overtones; it means "vulture" in German.

32. Heinimann, *Technische Innovation,* 226.

relationship between technology and superstition that he does in his essay "Die religiöse Bedeutung der Wissenschaft." In both works myth and technology are shown to be twins in a third-culture sense; separating the two would mean the death of both.[33]

Take the case of Seraphine's arsenic addiction. Geier has been supplying her with the poison and has led her to believe that a daily dose will keep her beautiful and strong. If she stops eating the toxin on a regular basis, her appearance will decline rapidly. The narrator tells us in a footnote that "In den Alpenländern findet sich dieser Glauben ziemlich häufig und gibt es sehr viele Hüttenrauch(Arsenik)esser [sic]. Besonders unter den Fuhrleuten, welche auch ihren Pferden zum Behufe der Kräftigung Arsenik geben, ist das Hüttenrauchessen gang und gäbe" (In the Alps such beliefs are quite common. There are many arsenic eaters. Arsenic eating is especially common among coach drivers, who also feed it to their horses for strength, NB 32). Thus Seraphine leads a tortured existence. She despises Geier yet depends on him for her beauty and strength. Enter Bruno Lechner.

Rosegger establishes the characters of Lechner and Geier as opposites. Lechner is the man of science and technology, and Geier is the archetype of superstitious man. As Lechner and Seraphine find themselves falling in love, she is forced to admit her dilemma. Certain that she will lose Lechner's love, she dejectedly proclaims, "So sag ich's rundweg: Eine Hüttenrauchesserin bin ich!" (I'll just say it outright: I am an arsenic eater! NB 67). Lechner functions as the agent of disillusion, the disenchanter of myth and superstition. He comforts Seraphine with the new faith of the nineteenth century—science, which disenchants and thus mollifies and comforts. Lechner realizes that Seraphine is a slave to superstition. He knows that arsenic in small amounts has no long-lasting detrimental effects. And he

---

33. Rosegger, "Religiöse Bedeutung," 148.

recognizes that the border between truth and superstition is not always clear. Science is Lechner's truth, and just as Geier inspires Seraphine's faith through superstition, Lechner attempts to comfort her through the power of science. He assures her of the chemical nature of arsenic and tells her, "Sie haben hier nichts als ein Vorurteil zu überwinden, das sich aus Ihrer Umgebung in Ihr Wesen eingewurzelt hat; das ist überwunden, wenn Sie mir glauben können" (You have only to overcome a superstition from your region that is deeply rooted in your being; if you can have faith in me, you can overcome it, *NB* 70). All Seraphine needs to do is to put her faith in his science, and she will conquer her problem. Faith is the key word here. Lechner cannot fully explain the science behind arsenic to Seraphine, so she must simply have faith in him. The point is that belief in science requires a nonscientific foundation—it requires faith just as much as belief in the deity requires faith—thereby restoring the "twin-like" nature of these two realms.

The close relationship between myth and technology also shows itself with regard to the train. When the first locomotive finally arrives in the village, the narrator, in a description that presages the train in Hauptmann's *Bahnwärter Thiel (The Linesman Thiel)* (1888), creates an image from the perspective of the villagers:

Ein Dröhnen und leises Beben im Boden und die Maschine brauste heran und wuchs zusehends, und das Schnauben wurde lauter und das hohe, schwarze Unding ging mit all seinem wunderbaren Anhang schwer und langsam in den Bahnhof. Diese mächtigen Eisenräder rollten glatt und gleich auf dem Geleise, man sah es ihnen an, daß sie in eherner Ruhe alles zermalmten, was sich ihnen etwa entgegenstellen mochte. Mehrere gewaltige Arme aus Eisen gingen aus dem Riesenkörper hervor und trieben die Räder. Aus dem hohen, gähnenden Schlunde qualmte schwarzer Rauch.

With a roar and quiet rumbling in the earth, the train thundered toward the crowd, and as it got closer and the snorting became louder, the massive black monstrosity with all of its wonderful cars came heavily and slowly into the train station. The powerful iron wheels rolled smoothly and evenly on the rails; one could see in them the ironclad ability to crush anything that stood in their way. Several enormous arms of iron that drove the wheels jutted out of the gigantic body. Out of its high, yawning maw blew black smoke. (*NB* 142)

This is no simple technological manifestation of science. This is a manifestation of the supernatural; it is a beast or a monster straight out of the mythological realm. From this description and from the numerous times the train is associated with the devil, it is clear that the people have already invested this new aspect of material reality with a good deal of myth.

Just as he did with the arsenic, Lechner understands that it is his task to disabuse the people of such notions, that is, to disenchant the train. But in this endeavor he ultimately fails. He assures the people that "unser heutiges Werk kommt nicht von gestern" (our modern [technological] work does not come from the past, *NB* 103). In other words, the train is something entirely new that does not rely on the old for its existence—a dubious proposition from either a physical or a metaphysical standpoint. He tells the people, "ich werde euch ... die Maschine und das ganze Wesen des Dampfwagens zeigen und erklären.... Mit dem Verständnisse des Systems habt ihr alles gewonnen; vorurteilsfrei werdet ihr zur Eisenbahn in günstiges, euch vorteilhaftes Verhältnis treten" (I will show and explain to you ... the entire essence of the steam locomotive.... With an understanding of the system you will be a winner, you will be able to approach the railway without prejudice, and you will enter into a positive and advantageous relationship with the train, *NB* 105). The engineer will thus explain, show, and name so that fears may be allayed. Naming, explaining, and identifying are the processes by which science derives its power, and, paradoxically, by which myth derives its power as well.

The problem is that Lechner cannot "disenchant" the train itself. He does all of his explaining prior to the trial run only to convince people of the need for a railway in the valley. All of the naming and explaining that is supposed to demonstrate the power of science comes to naught. For after the trial run, Lechner himself admits, "Wir verstehen es . . . nur halb . . . wir haben die Kraft entdeckt und sie für unsere menschlichen Zwecke anzuwenden gelernt, wer jedoch könnte sagen, was diese Kraft ist?" (We understand it . . . only halfway . . . we discovered the power and have learned to use it for our purposes. Who, however, could say just what this power is? *NB* 149). This is the border to which Rosegger refers in "Religiöse Bedeutung der Wissenschaft." It is not, therefore, the border that divides us from an unknown that we should fear, but the border that divides a realm explained solely through Christianity, according to Rosegger. Following Adorno and Horkheimer, this is yet another example of the myth that underlies enlightenment and the enlightenment that underlies myth. That is, the myth of an absolute has granted this power, and this power in turn allows us a glimpse of the absolute.

One also sees this dichotomy in the way the narrator continually mythologizes Lechner, the man of technology. His riding in on a mechanical steed, bringing the fire equipment from the nearby city and saving the village, is one instance of this. There is also the verse from a song Lechner sings as the train begins to move out on its trial run:

> Da kam ein fremder Ritter ins Land
> Und warb um der Prinzessin Hand;
> Er warb umsonst;—die Lieb' war groß,
> Er schwang die Maid auf sein hohes Roß
> Und hat sie entführt—.
> There came a strange knight into the land
> And sued he did for the princess's hand;
> He sued in vain—his love was great,
> He swung the maiden on his high steed
> And carried her off—.
>
> *(NB 146)*

The man who would disenchant equates himself, the technician, with a knight and his technological wonder with a steed. This is not necessarily proof that Lechner understands the human need for both a scientific and a mythological narrative, but it is nonetheless an example of how technology can ultimately become its own myth.

The Postmaster points this out succinctly in a conversation with Lechner after the trial run. He believes that his generation will never understand some of these new technologies that are changing the face of civilization. The old must learn from the young: "Nu ja, von einer . . . Enkelschar dürften wir uns noch dann und wann erzählen lassen, wie's zugeht in der neuen, wunderlichen Welt. Wenn sonst die Alten den Jungen Märchen erzählt haben, so mag es jetzt umgekehrt sein" (Well, our grandchildren will have to tell us now and then about the latest in this new, wondrous world. Once upon a time, the old told the young fairytales; now it could be just the opposite, *NB* 158). The older generation will learn the fairytale about Lechner, the knight who rode into town, saved them from obsolescence and possible destruction, and ultimately married the princess. In another story, they will hear about the Lechner whom the villagers revered as their savior and to whom they attributed their "reines, süßes Seelenglück" (pure, sweet happiness of their souls, *NB* 162). They must learn from the young that there are grand new fairytales that will ultimately be associated with the new technologies. Twenty-two years later, however, the fairytales associated with the train will take a decidedly darker turn in Rosegger's novel of the transition of a rural Alpine village into the modern world.

Das ewige Licht

Das ewige Licht is a very different work from *Die neue Bahn* in many ways. Most obviously, it is an epistolary novel rather than a novella. In addition, the scientists and technicians in its pages are few and far between. *Das ewige Licht* focuses primarily on the reaction of farmers and the clergy to the new spirit of progress that reigned in late nineteenth-century Austria. A final and most important difference is that the train does not bring the kind of benefits promised by Bruno Lechner in *Die neue Bahn*. To the contrary, not only does the train in *Das ewige Licht* add nothing positive to the village of Torwald, but its arrival heralds the demise of the village. When the train finally comes to Torwald, the village falls headlong into chaos.

In this work Rosegger depicts the unraveling of an individual, as well as of a society and a way of life. Through diary entries, with which Rosegger creates an illusion of reality, he relates the story of Wolfgang Wieser, a young progressive pastor who, as penance for his inappropriately provocative writings on Catholicism, is given a parish in Torwald, an out-of-the-way village high in the Alps.[34] He is sent there to replace the former priest, who went insane and died in an asylum, and to revitalize the parish. Wieser shepherds his flock admirably in the eyes of the Church authorities and becomes less progressive in his view of Catholicism.[35] From his new parishioners he learns the importance of old-fashioned Catholic values. Just as he is undergoing this transformation, however, the progressive ethic reappears in the form of a newcomer to the village, Josef Freiherr Ritter von Yark. Yark, a converted Jew, uses his wealth to modernize the town, first through tourism and then through industry. This industrial progress proves to be the undoing of the town and all it has stood for since time immemorial. It also, ironically, brings the downfall of the formerly progressive Wolfgang Wieser.

After we learn of Wieser's troubles with the Church author-

---

34. Karl Wagner, *Die literarische Öffentlichkeit der Provinzliteratur: Der Volksschriftsteller Peter Rosegger* (Tübingen: Niemeyer, 1991), 334.

35. All *Licht* excerpts are from Peter Rosegger, *Das ewige Licht* (1895) (Munich: L. Staackmann, n.d.).

ities as a liberal young priest, we accompany Wieser on his journey to Torwald. He takes the train to the end of the line, some distance from Torwald, and he writes of his rail journey, "Das ist gut auf den geräuschvollen Bahnhöfen und über den dröhnenden Rädern, es kommt nicht viel Herzweh auf, man hat keine Zeit dazu. Es ist ein Einschläfern in diesen Wiegen für große Kinder.—Draußen auf der Ebene, ja freilich, dort steht schon das Korn in Ähren, hier blühen die Obstbäume" (It is good to be in the noisy train stations and on the roaring wheels. One has no time for heartache. These cradles for overgrown children induce sleep.—Of course, outside the wheat is ready for harvest and the fruit trees are blossoming, EL 12). This passage suggests the role that the railway plays in this novel. Despite the great noise associated with the train, its rhythmic motion has a soporific effect. Wieser mentions the coming of the rail to Torwald throughout the work, usually in a subtle way. The first mention comes in an entry dated 1875, in which he notes that the blacksmith, the leader of the village, bemoans the draining away of the region's youth, who have left in great numbers to work on the railway or in factories. In 1878, Wieser writes, "Das Stift ist jetzt in froher Aufregung der neuen Eisenbahn wegen, die gebaut wird mit der Endstation Alpenzell" (the monastery is now happily excited because the new railway will come all the way to the town of Alpenzell, EL 122). In an entry in 1883 he worries, "Es wird nicht lange mehr dauern mit den Kutschen. Durch das Tal herein über aufgewühlte Erdwälle und Dämme, über Eisenbrücken ist eine schnurgerade Linie gezogen, Wiesen sind überschüttet, der Wald ist durchbrochen, Erdarbeiten, Stangen, Baracken . . . vom Keilerstein bis Oberschuttbach" (The horse-drawn carriages won't last much longer. Iron tracks have drawn a straight line through the valley over churned-up earth. They have overrun meadows, broken through the forest—earthworks, metal rods, barracks . . . from Keilerstein to Oberschuttbach, EL 174). In 1884 he notes that the coming of the train has turned his otherwise naïve, innocent maid, Ottilie, into a technician who can name all the parts of a train (*EL* 182). Finally, in September 1884, the train arrives.

In contrast to the role repetition plays in Auerbach's works, Rosegger's understated repetition is innocuous and has the same "cradling" effect as does the train itself. In her analysis of repetition, Johnstone suggests that one of the things it does is to put off that which people fear.[36] This is how Rosegger employs the railway repetition in *Das ewige Licht*. The reader, like the villagers in Torwald, grows so used to the idea that the rail is on the way by the time it finally arrives the fear has largely abated. Even in the culminating scene, when the train pulls in to Torwald station, Wieser proclaims, "Zum Leutverderben kommt der Dampfwagen ja freilich schon zu spät. Vor etlichen Jahren, wenn 'das [*sic*] Lokomotiv' so gekommen ware, würde ich wahrscheinlich ganz evangelisch gesagt haben: Der Wolf fährt in die Schafherde!" (The train has come too late to corrupt the people. Many years ago, if the locomotive were to have come as it has now, I would have evangelically stated: The wolf has been loosed among the flock! *EL* 196). He is right that the people have already been corrupted in the course of the novel, but, as will become clear in the remainder of the work, Wieser has been cradled to sleep as well. He never fully understands the nature of the wolf or the extent of the damage yet to be wrought on his flock.

A look at Wieser's final appearance in conjunction with the rail stands in great contrast to his first trip to Torwald by rail. It also emphasizes his fundamental misunderstanding of the type of progress the railway brings with it. After he has left the parish, he roams the region in something like a schizophrenic haze, and he is seen now and then in the meadows of Unterschuttbach and on the rail embankments. This contrasts nicely with the passage describing that first trip by rail—the images of the cradle-train and the fertile fields ready for harvest. Whereas we first saw him

---

36. Johnstone, *Repetition in Discourse*, 13.

securely ensconced inside the cradle-train, he roams the now desolate fields that he first viewed from the train window. And instead of the image of the train as the cradle, we have the train as an agitator intellectually and spiritually hounding a man to an ignominious death in full view of the train embankment. This is the result of Wieser's having been lulled to sleep by the train.

In order to understand the village's demise as depicted between the two contrasting railway images that frame this work, one must first analyze the scene depicting Wieser's arrival in Torwald, which at the time was not accessible by train. In 1875 the only way to reach the tiny village was by foot, through a cave pass known as the "Wurmlucken" (Worm Gap, *EL* 22). This scene is full of birth imagery. Upon exiting the tunnel, one is born into a "freie, weite lichte Landschaft" (wide open light landscape) where, "in ziemlicher Entfernung auf einem steilen bewaldeten Hügel die schlanke Nadel eines Kirchturms [ragte]" (in the distance, on a steep, forested hilltop, the thin needle of a church tower [rose] up, *EL* 22). A virtual rebirth is what the Church authorities required of Wieser, and a rebirth is what they get. Authors like Rousseau and Geßner, whom he studied in the past, are like mummies to him now. Wieser believes that God has finally led him to his idyll. He is thus reborn into a virtual Eden protected from the vagaries of the world by its geography and its faith.

While the physical manifestation of the town is protected geographically by the Wurmlucken, its faith is protected by the church as it sits on high. And just as the Wurmlucken will be destroyed to make way for the train, so too will the church. A thick, fortress-like wall surrounds Wieser's new church, an image very similar to the fortress ruins in *Sträflinge*. The key difference is that the fortress in *Sträflinge* is reconciled with the railway, and through this reconciliation the reader encounters the linesman's beautiful house. The church fortress in *Das ewige Licht* will never peacefully accommodate the railway or any other new technology.

After the profiteer Yark determines that the region is no longer profitable as a tourist area, he makes the shift to mining. The village, in an effort to raise funds, sells Yark the land around the church. He wastes no time in removing the valuable rust-colored ore from the church grounds. The train literally undermines the church and figuratively undermines the villagers' faith.[37] Later Wieser writes, "An sechs oder sieben Seiten ist der Kirchenriegel abgegraben" (The church's wall has been excavated on six or seven sides, *EL* 225), and the train continues to destroy its foundation. Finally, the building itself is damaged. "Ein schwarzes scharfes Schricklein, das vom Fenster gegen den Boden herabgeht, ein ganz dünner, feiner Sprung" (A black, sharp crack develops from a window down to the floor, a very thin, fine break, *EL* 248). In the next entry Wieser notes more cracks filled with dust and bugs near the tower and the baptismal font. This tower, which proudly welcomed Wieser to Torwald fourteen years earlier, now stands cracked and decaying. The damage comes dangerously close to the baptismal font, a symbol of faith against the forces of evil. Even given all of this evidence, Wieser still does not understand how the damage is occurring. "Es hat keine Gefahr.—Wenn ich nur wüßte, welche Ursache solche Sprünge haben" (There is no danger.—If I only knew what the cause of these breaks was! *EL* 248). Thus Wieser's idyllic fortress is besieged and gradually destroyed by modernizing forces like the train, and he has been lulled to the point where he cannot even understand why.

Although he is blind to the causes, Wieser's demise and that of the region become obvious to the reader through several in-

---

37. It will not be lost on the reader that Yark, who sets the train in motion to undermine the church, is a converted Jew. Rosegger's decision to make a Jew the embodiment of corrupt modernization is most certainly antisemitic. More than one critic has made this charge. As with many other aspects of Rosegger's worldview, however, his anti-Semitism is not always clear. As a counterexample, I offer his unequivocal praise of Berthold Auerbach and his work.

stances of foreshadowing, two of which are particularly ominous. First, as Wieser is moving into his new quarters, he finds a diary written by his predecessor, Johann Steinberger. Rosegger gives us here a diary within a diary read by Wieser. In Steinberger's diary Wieser learns of an event that may have pushed his predecessor over the edge. Steinberger is faced with the situation of a man wrongfully condemned to death for murder. He knows that this man is innocent because the real murderer told him so during a confession. Torn by his vow of confidentiality, Steinberger confronts the murderer and persuades him to go and confess to the court. But they arrive too late, and the innocent man is hanged.

Most of Steinberger's travels during this episode take place by train, and it is his view of the train that is of interest here. He writes in his diary:

Am Abend des zweiten Tages bin ich im Liesgau, wo sie die Eisenbahn bauen. Da geht's zu! Die ganze Gegend wenden sie um wie einen alten Rock; schon bald wie es in der Heiligen Schrift heißt: Jedes Tal soll ausgefüllet, jeder Hügel soll abgetragen werden, was krumm ist, soll gerade, was uneben ist, zu einem ebenen Wege werden. Aber der Heiland, der kommen soll, auf den bin ich gar nicht neugierig.

On the evening of the second day, I am in Liesgau, where they are building the railway. It's coming together here. They're changing the whole region like an old skirt; soon, as it says in the holy Bible: Every valley will be filled in, every hilltop leveled, that which is crooked will be made straight, that which is uneven will be made even. But I am not the least bit curious regarding the kind of savior who is supposedly coming. (*EL* 70)

This passage has two functions. First, it foreshadows what is to happen to the valley of Torwald. The valley is transformed, and the "savior" who comes is technological progress in the form of the train. Given the ironic understatement of the last line of this passage, it becomes clear that Steinberger associates the train with Satan, or at the very least with evil. When he makes this equation and claims that the Bible calls for this, he is mythologizing the origins of technology. In other words, out of the myth of the Bible comes this technology, and in this way the train can become a part of the greater narrative that helps the villagers deal with what they do not completely understand—that is, why their region is declining in so many ways.

The other half of the Adorno-Horkheimer dialectic—which says that technology will produce its own myth—is also addressed in this passage. Although the railway is still in its infancy, Steinberger suggests that it will bring with it an evil savior. Technology will produce its own myth of evil. This view stands in great contrast to the positive mythological function the train serves in "Der Dorfbahnhof" and in Auerbach's work. In fact, in a diary passage written in 1886, Wieser dismisses the notion that the train will bring goodness in any form: "Seit die Eisenbahn geht, könne keine Hungersnot mehr kommen, heißt es. Bisher hat die Eisenbahn nicht einen einzigen Sack Korn hereingebracht für den, der ihn nicht kaufen könnte" (They say that with the advent of the railway, no one will go hungry. Up to now, the railway has not brought one single sack of wheat for those too poor to pay for it, *EL* 209). The train is not capable of such virtuous and Christ-like deeds as feeding the masses. It is, however, capable of destroying the virtue of charity, as Wieser points out in the very next sentence: "Und geteilt . . . wird auch nicht mehr" (And sharing . . . doesn't happen anymore either).

The second ominous example of foreshadowing related to Steinberger's remarks on the train occurs in a passage written in 1878. Wieser writes, "manchmal schreckt mich etwas auf, als wäre durch die Luft ein Ungetüm geflattert. Als ob etwas Unerhörtes kommen müsse über unser Torwaldtal. Ein Bergsturz am Beilerstein? Eine Sündflut?—Torheiten. Die Sündflut hat draußen in der weiten Welt bequemer Platz. Unser Alpental soll eine Arche sein" (at times something frightens me, as if something monstrous were fluttering through the air. As if something unheard of were to come over our valley of Torwald. A rockslide in Beilerstein? An Old Testament flood?—Foolishness. That type

Das ewige Licht 81

of flood would have more room out in the wider world. Our Alpine valley shall be an ark, *EL* 115). The flood directly relates these thoughts to those of Steinberger, whose unholy savior is related to Wieser's "Ungetüm" (something monstrous) and "Unerhörtes" (something unheard of). With these terms, which give the train a frightening, supernatural air, Rosegger hearkens back to Heine's vision of the train and Hauptmann's depiction of it in *Bahnwärter Thiel*.

Evil is the mythology that the train reinforces throughout the work. Nowhere is this more evident than when the train finally arrives in Torwald on September 6, 1884. Wieser writes, "Wir sind mit zwei eisernen Strängen angeschmiedet an die große Welt. Die Schienen, diese eisernen Dopplestriche, sind das Gleichungszeichen der Menschheit, hörte ich einmal sagen" (We have been forged to the wide world with two iron bands. I heard it said once that the tracks, these double iron lines, are the symbol of human equality, *EL* 195). Although he highlights here some of the "Listian" advantages of the rail—as the carrier of culture and democratizing agent—he does so with understated skepticism. Then the "schwarze Ungetüm" ("black monster") comes, and he describes it as "nicht bloß ein Sehen, es ist ein Erleben, es gräbt sich ins Hirn wie ein Schicksal, es ändert das Blut" (not merely a sight, it is an experience, it burrows into your brain like destiny, it changes your blood, *EL* 195). Thus we are given the train as destiny. To be sure, inasmuch as images like burrowing into the brain and changing one's blood are not positive, the destiny represented by the train is a frightening one. Its dark connotations are further supported by the villagers' reactions: "Tuts beten, daß er nicht kommt!" (Pray that it doesn't come!); "Der höllisch Drach, jetzt ist er da" (The hellish dragon, now it is here, *EL* 195). The villagers fear that the train will bring them hell on earth—not yet reality but fearful speculation.

But the predictions appear to come true with the death of Gralin, the oldest resident of the village. She spends the entire morning of the arrival of the train telling of prophecies that she heard in her childhood. "[E]s wird einmal eine Zeit kommen, da werden sie den Himmelsblitz auf Stangen hängen und eiserne Straßen bauen. Und dann werden feuerspeiende Drachen kommen, so groß, daß siebenmal sieben Reiter darauf können reiten. Und dann kommt das Ende der Welt" (there will come a time when they will hang lightning on rods and build iron streets. And then the fire-spewing dragons will come, so big that seven times seven riders can sit atop them. And then comes the end of the world, *EL* 196). Finally the train comes, and her seventy-seven-year-old son urges her to leave Torwald. "'Jetzt?'" she replies. "'Dummer Bub, jetzt wird's erst lustig!' Wie sie das gesagt hat, sinkt sie zurück an die Wand, und wie wir sie fragen wollen, was sie hat—da lebt sie nicht mehr. . . . Bald wissen es alle, viele finden die Mär noch seltsamer als den Einzug des Dampfrosses. Hundert und so viel Jahre! Man hat gar nicht mehr gedacht, daß sie sterben wird" ("Now? Silly boy, now the fun is about to begin!" Having said that, she sinks back against the wall, and when we try to ask her what is wrong—she's no longer alive. . . . Soon all know of her death and many find the story stranger than the arrival of the train. One hundred plus years! No one had thought she would ever die, *EL* 196). Metaphorically, the train has killed the oldest living resident of a region that was protected for centuries, through faith and geography, from the dangers of the modern world. The other important aspect of this passage is that the story of the death of Gralin has already become a legend or, in German, a *Mär*. While not quite yet a fairy tale, or *Märchen,* one can see that it is headed in this direction because the *Mär* of Gralin's death is so closely linked with the *Mär* of the train's arrival. Here Rosegger makes the twin-like relationship between technology and myth very clear.

Gralin's death is one of Rosegger's final fictional statements on the railway, and the reader is left with a typically ambivalent image. In *Die neue Bahn,* Rosegger lauds the railway as a cultural savior, while in *Das ewige Licht* he decries it as a destroyer of an older, more moral age. The fact that *Die neue Bahn* and *Das ewige Licht* were written twenty-two years apart explains the discrepancy in part. In industrialism, Rosegger felt that he witnessed over the years the undoing of a way of life in the Styrian region of Austria, yet he never hesitated to take advantage of his free first-class rail pass. Regardless of this seeming contradiction, Rosegger did understand and demonstrate in his work, both fiction and nonfiction, that myth and science are part of one story; there is no avoiding their "twin-like" nature. In their attempts to come to terms with the natural and the supernatural world, myth and science are not opposites but mirror images of each other.

[4]

THEODOR FONTANE

Aus einem edlen Stamme
  Sproß er, der Junker Dampf:
Das Wasser und die Flamme,
  Sie zeugten ihn im Kampf

Of noble origins
  He sprang, the squire steam:
The water and the flame,
  They forged him in struggle

Theodor Fontane, "Der Junker Dampf" (The Squire Steam) *(1887)*

Theodor Fontane was born in Neuruppin near Berlin in 1819, more than twenty-five years before the first steam-driven German railway, the Bavarian Nürnberg-Fürth line, was built.[1] By 1878, when Fontane published *Vor dem Sturm (Before the Storm)*, his first major work of fiction, the German railway system was flourishing. For him, the rail was therefore not something startlingly new.[2] Unlike the Heines of the world, Fontane did not perceive an uncanny horror or monster in the

---

1. James M. Brophy, *Capitalism, Politics, and Railroads in Prussia, 1830–1870* (Columbus: Ohio State University Press, 1998), 24.

2. In fact, Fontane contributed to a journal called *Die Eisenbahn (The*

train.³ But this does not mean that Heinimann is right to diminish the importance of the railway in Fontane's works by suggesting that it had been already assimilated into literature by the time Fontane was writing. Heinimann takes this argument too far when he suggests that, for Fontane, the relationship between man, technology, and nature was no longer problematic.⁴ Fontane certainly does look at this relationship, but he does so in a very different way from Rosegger and Auerbach. Literary representations of technology in Fontane are often unobtrusive and even hidden.⁵ With the possible exception of one scene in *Cécile,* the train is never depicted as dramatically as it is in the works of Rosegger and Auerbach. It is never the fiery dragon or the iron devil.

This does not mean that the train is a less important device in the works of Fontane. He is yet another author who tried to accommodate the old and the new, and he could not help seeing the relationship between man, technology, and nature as problematic. It may seem odd to be discussing myth in the work of an acclaimed realist like Fontane, but he does frequently rely on ghost stories, fairytales, Wagner operas, and so on. As a realist he is supposed to scorn romantic or idealized notions, but he never does so entirely. In fact, notions like these are often closely related to literary devices like the railway in his work. As Segeberg correctly points out, the train in *Effi Briest* plays a role similar to that of Instetten's Asian ghost.⁶ Thus Mahr seems off base when he surmises that nineteenth-century authors encountered irresolvable conflicts when they tried to depict new technological innovations within older imaginative constructs and the lan-

---

Railway)—a liberal journal so named mainly for the modernistic sound of *Eisenbahn* rather than for its direct connection with the railway.

3. See Heine, *Sämtliche Werke,* 4:57–58.

4. Heinimann, *Technische Innovation,* 19.

5. Harro Segeberg, *Literatur im technischen Zeitalter: Von der Frühzeit der Deutschen Aufklärung bis zum Beginn des Ersten Weltkriegs* (Darmstadt: Wissenschaftliche Buchgesellschaft, 1997), 176.

6. Ibid., 177.

guage of the past.⁷ If Mahr were correct, Fontane would have had to abandon the three witches in his poem "Die Brück' am Tay" (The Bridge over the Tay) (1880), the Place of the Witch's Dance in his novel *Cécile* (1887), and the ghost in *Effi Briest* (1895), but to abandon these was to abandon the familiar narrative. Fontane apparently saw no irresolvable conflict in depicting these mythical figures in a work of realism. In fact, the resolution of this apparent conflict is the essence of Fontane's realist aesthetic.

Fontane's Realism

The crux of Fontane's aesthetic lies in his concept of *Verklärung* (transfiguration), an idea, according to Hugo Aust, that Fontane embraced as a literary antidote taken to prevent literature from sinking to the level of the scientific essay.⁸ In his programmatic 1853 essay "Unsere epische und lyrische Poesie seit 1848" (Our Epic and Lyric Poetry since 1848), Fontane often used the metaphor of raw materials to express this aspect of his literary theory. In an implicit critique of Young Germany and a prefiguration of naturalism, he wrote, "Vor allen Dingen verstehen wir *nicht* darunter [realismus] das nackte Wiedergeben alltäglichen Lebens, am wenigsten seines Elends und seiner Schattenseiten. . . . Es ist noch nicht allzu lange her, daß man . . . bei Darstellung eines sterbenden Proletariers, den hungernde Kinder umstehen . . . sich einbildete, der Kunst eine glänzende Richtung vorgezeichnet zu haben" (Above all, we do *not* understand realism as the bare replication of everyday life, especially not with its misery and its shadowy underbelly. . . . Not long ago, some thought that the depiction of a dying proletarian sur-

---

7. Mahr, *Eisenbahnen in der deutschen Dichtung*, 160.
8. Hugo Aust, *Theodor Fontane: "Verklärung,"* in *Eine Untersuchung zum Ideengehalt seiner Werke* (Bonn: Bouvier, 1974), 20.

rounded by his children paved the way for a shining new direction in art). The depiction of "bare reality" bears the same relation to realism as "das rohe Erz zum Metall . . . die Läuterung fehlt" (ore to metal . . . it lacks refinement).[9] In his review of Paul Lindau's novel *Der Zug nach dem Westen (The Train West)* (1886), Fontane echoed Rosegger's refusal to depict reality where it is most ugly,[10] rejecting the works of Fritz Mauthner and Max Kretzer as too dependent on the misery of human existence. These works lacked reconciliation, mildness, good cheer, and nature.[11] The antidote was *Verklärung* (transfiguration), which Fontane made clear again in his metaphor of the marble quarry: "Das Leben ist doch immer nur der Marmorsteinbruch, der den Stoff zu unendlichen Bildwerken in sich trägt; sie schlummern darin, aber nur dem Auge des Geweihten sichtbar und nur durch seine Hand zu erwecken" (Life is like a marble quarry carrying in it endless material for sculptures slumbering within. But they are only apparent to the eye of the knowing artist and can only be awakened by his hand).[12] It was the artist's task to transfigure some aspect of reality by making it aesthetically pleasing and true. Only then could a work of literature achieve a degree of reconciliation, an idea that anticipates Auerbach's 1879 essay "Ein Tag in der Heimat."[13]

Two aspects of Fontane's theory are striking. The first is that transfiguration involves a breaking down of reality. The second, paradoxically, is that transfiguration involves a building up of reality. In choosing the block of marble, the artist is breaking down an aspect of bare everyday life, that is, he is breaking down the quarry. His job then is to transfigure it, to build it back up

9. Fontane, "Unsere epische und lyrische Poesie," 240–41.
10. Rosegger, "Alte und neue Schönheit," 442.
11. Theodor Fontane, *"Der Zug nach dem Westen,"* in *Aufsätze, Kritiken, Erinnerungen,* ed. Jürgen Kolbe, sec. 3, vol. 1 of *Sämtliche Werke,* ed. Walter Keitel (Munich: Hanser, 1969), 569.
12. Fontane, "Unsere epische und lyrische Poesie," 241.
13. Fontane, *"Zug nach dem Westen,"* 569.

into an aesthetic whole. D. A. Williams writes, "The Realist aims at being as complete and comprehensive as possible, at totalizing as well as miniaturizing the real."[14] The block itself is too real, and Helen Chambers argues that a writer who attempts to depict reality "as it is" ends up with a work that is paradoxically unreal.[15] Fontane was of course aware of the absurdity of the notion of art as a "literal" representation of reality, a preposterous, oxymoronic notion by definition, since the mere fact of *representation* necessarily alters that "reality."

Recall that Adorno and Horkheimer argue that the essence of art is that the general is conveyed in the particular.[16] The block of marble gives the appearance of the quarry, but it is not identical to the quarry. Bare, everyday life is what they claim the Enlightenment program purports to represent. Myth provides the transfiguration. The dialectic of the two allows for art; it allows Fontane to put the Chinese ghost in *Effi Briest* and the enchanted castle in *Cécile,* and to relate both so closely to the train. As Downing points out, "the mythical ... represents for [Adorno and Horkheimer] an acknowledgment of otherness, difference, or alterity." What is key to Downing's statement is that myth is also an expression of power located outside the empirical realm, and the process of mimesis "is understood as an attempt ... to participate in and so to acquire some of that power."[17] Mimesis, then, is power that is wrapped up in both enlightenment and myth, and, as we shall see in *Cécile* and *Effi Briest,* both of these realms are conveyed by the train.

---

14. D. A. Williams, *The Monster in the Mirror: Studies in Nineteenth-Century Realism* (Oxford: Oxford University Press, 1980), 258.

15. Helen Elizabeth Chambers, *Supernatural and Irrational Elements in the Works of Theodor Fontane* (Stuttgart: Heinz, 1980), 84.

16. Adorno and Horkheimer, *Dialectic of Enlightenment,* 25.

17. Downing, *Double Exposures,* 8.

Cécile

We see an interesting example of this dynamic at work in Fontane's 1887 novel *Cécile*.[18] Fontane summarized the essence of this work in a letter to Adolph Glaser: "Ein forscher Kerl, 35, Mann von Welt, liebt und verehrt—nein verehrt ist zu viel—liebt und umcourt eine schöne junge Frau, kränklich, pikant. Eines schönen Tages entpuppt sie sich als reponierte Fürstengeliebte. Sofort veränderter Ton, Zudringlichkeit mit den Allüren des guten Rechts. Konflikte; tragischer Ausgang" (A forceful fellow, 35, man of the world, loves and worships—no, worships is too much—loves and courts a pretty young woman, sickly, piquant. One fine day she turns out to be a former mistress of a prince. Immediate change in tone, liberties are taken. Conflicts; tragic outcome).[19] The worldly young man is Robert von Gordon-Leslie, a civil engineer and cable expert. The young woman is Cécile, the beautiful former mistress of a prince. Shortly before their marriage, her much older husband, Pierre St. Arnaud, fought and won a duel over Cécile's honor. Because of their checkered past, the couple is generally shunned by polite Berlin society. While on vacation in Thale in the Harz Mountains, Gordon falls in love with Cécile. He is forced to leave early on business and never confesses his feelings for her. During his absence, Gordon's sister writes him a letter that satisfies his curiosity regarding Cécile's past. Upon learning these details, he feels justified in taking certain liberties with Cécile, which she thoroughly rejects. After St. Arnaud learns of one such incident, which takes place in public at the opera, he demands satisfaction from Gordon and kills him in a duel—not out of love for his wife, for he is most often a neglectful, mean-spirited husband, but rather out of pride.

18. All references to *Cécile* are from *Romane, Erzählungen, Gedichte*, sec. 1, vol. 2 of *Sämtliche Werke*, ed. Walter Keitel (Munich: Hanser 1962), 141–317.

19. Fontane to Adolph Glaser, quoted in Hermann Korte, *Ordnung und Tabu: Studien zum poetischen Realismus* (Bonn: Bouvier, 1989), 102.

Fontane's use of the railway as a repetitive symbol is a key to understanding this social novel. The train is first used in the opening of the novel as Cécile and St. Arnaud depart Berlin for Thale, and the entire opening chapter consists of a depiction of their railway journey. The clock tower in the train station in Thale is juxtaposed with a conversation between the St. Arnauds and Gordon regarding an apparently enchanted castle. The speed with which the train transports the group from Thale to Quedlinburg brings to an end their argument about the efficacy of "old" stories. Cécile is enchanted by the view out the windows of this train. At dinner one evening in Thale, Gordon and St. Arnaud have a rather strange, comical discussion that foreshadows their ultimate conflict. The discussion contrasts those who enjoy having the windows open on a train and those who do not. On a walk with St. Arnaud in Thale, Cécile's daydreams are interrupted by the crossing signal and the whistle of the locomotive, which is contrasted with a mass of yellow butterflies that catch her attention. A train in the valley coming from Quedlinburg and the Devil's Wall punctuates a lengthy monologue held by St. Arnaud regarding the entire Harz region as witch country. The final three images of the train are associated with Gordon. He sits backward on the early train from Thale and contemplates the *Roßtrappe,* a distinct geographical feature named for the legend of a princess whose giant horse left a hoof print on a peak in the region, the *Hexentanzplatz* (Place of the Witches' Dance), while musing on his relationship with Cécile. On his way by foot to Cécile's house in Berlin, his journey is disrupted by the construction of a rail crossing. And finally, the Dresden Express takes Gordon to his death.

It is clear that repetition plays a significant role in the way Fontane employs the train as a literary device in *Cécile*. Johnstone's analysis of repetition in language is once more relevant, especially her suggestion that repetition helps people deal with the unknown or the misunderstood.[20] Both mythological and

---

20. Johnstone, *Repetition in Discourse,* 13.

scientific narratives attempt to allay human fears, and this effort is the key to understanding Fontane's depiction of the train. All three elements of Johnstone's discussion of repetition are present in *Cécile*. The train, an extension of the Enlightenment inasmuch as technology is the natural outcome of scientific experiment, is frequently juxtaposed with some form of myth, such as the fairytale. The train is also associated with Cécile's fear of social convention, of her past, and of her husband. In fact, her fear is one of the psychological forces that drives the plot.

The motif of fear and the associated desire to flee dominate the entire first chapter—and, as is so often the case with Fontane, the first chapter is the key to the rest of the novel. At the outset we are introduced to the St. Arnauds as they board the train for Thale. St. Arnaud is described as strong, whereas Cécile is described as a convalescent, thereby establishing their dominant characteristics. As the train gets under way, St. Arnaud says, "Gott sei Dank, Cécile ... Gott sei Dank, wir sind allein" ("Thank God, Cécile ... Thank God, we're alone, *C* 142). Clearly, leaving Berlin society is quite a relief to the couple.

Their status as outsiders to society is confirmed on a stop in one of the outlying areas of Berlin. The narrator explains that "Viele Militärs schritten hier den Perron auf und ab, unter ihnen auch ein alter General, der, als er Céciles ansichtig wurde, mit besonderer Artigkeit in das Coupé hinein grüßte, dann aber sofort vermied, abermals in die Nähe desselben zu kommen" (Many military men were walking back and forth on the platform, among them an old general, who, when he saw Cécile, greeted her with particular courtesy. Then, however, he immediately avoided getting close to her rail car again, *C* 142–43). This slight from a fellow former officer does not go unnoticed by either Cécile or St. Arnaud. St. Arnaud comments on the lack of independence these gentlemen show, implying that the general's natural desire to greet the couple was stifled by the pressure to conform to social convention. Thus far Heinimann is correct in his analysis of the scene. He calls the train a symbol of estrangement and notes that it is not simply a means of transportation but, for Cécile, the path to a carefree existence. Paradoxically, however, when the train later travels back to Berlin, it is the path to sorrow.[21] What Heinimann overlooks is that Cécile, and to some degree her husband, are afraid, and the basis of their fear is their sense of helplessness and powerlessness in the face of social ostracism. The beginning of the repetition is the clue to this. Cécile tells her husband, "Erzähl mir etwas Hübsches, etwas von Glück und Freude. Gibt es nicht eine Geschichte: Die Reise nach dem Glück? Oder ist es bloß ein Märchen?" (Tell me something nice, something about happiness and joy. Isn't there a story: The Journey to Happiness? Or is it merely a fairytale? C 144). St. Arnaud, much to Cécile's dismay, confirms that happiness is just a fairytale.

In his analysis of *Cécile,* Walter Müller-Seidel suggests that St. Arnaud is right, that there is no such thing as a real idyll, only fairytales.[22] Hence, with the discussion of fairytales and the train, we have the beginning of the juxtaposition of the railway and myth. And to drive this connection home, upon their arrival in Thale St. Arnaud tells Cécile that the Harz is receiving her like a princess (C 145). The train will never be disenchanted in this novel; it cannot be. Just as myth, through its process of repetition, recognizes uniqueness and otherness in man and nature, so too does enlightenment through its repetition. Thus she of the "dreamy and fairytale-like" disposition can, through her fear and her otherness, be repeatedly associated with the train and the fairytale, with both myth and enlightenment.

The association continues when Gordon and the St. Arnauds take a walk on the *Roßtrappe*. Here they come across a castle that Cécile describes as magical, like a castle from a fairytale in which both peace and happiness reign. Gordon, playing a

---

21. Heinimann, *Technische Innovation,* 238.
22. Walter Müller-Seidel, *Theodor Fontane: Soziale Romankunst in Deutschland* (Stuttgart: Metzler, 1975), 195.

role similar to that of Lechner in Rosegger's *Die neue Bahn,* takes it upon himself to disabuse her of this romantic notion. He tells the St. Arnauds a chilling story of suicide and a dark spirit that haunts the castle. This is another confirmation of St. Arnaud's reply to Cécile's wish for happiness: "Es wird wohl ein Märchen sein" (It is probably a fairytale, *C* 144); once again, the mythical is juxtaposed with the train. A long silence follows Gordon's remarks on the fairytale, interrupted by the clock tower in the train station down in Thale. Although Gordon's story is a rather obvious foreshadowing of the story's violent outcome, it also serves as another reminder of the dialectic between technology and myth.

Chambers, in her work on the supernatural in Fontane, points out that the supernatural emphasizes the apparent inevitability of events. Not that Fontane holds this view himself; it is how his characters sometimes deal with extraordinary events that evoke fear. They fear the inevitability of events caused not by supernatural forces but "by irrational, unbiddable forces inherent in the personalities of the characters and the society in which they live."[23] The repetitive nature of the supernatural references suggests their role in explaining things the characters do not understand. What Chambers misses is that Fontane does not just demonstrate this with his use of ghosts, fairytales, and the like, but also with a concrete empirical reality—the train. Thus the reason for the castle owner's suicide is explained with yet another of Fontane's ghost stories and punctuated by the ringing of the train station's clock tower. Both things, through their repetition, express the power that exists outside the human realm, and therefore highlight the sense of powerlessness Cécile feels in society's rejection.

The same point is made when a group that includes the St. Arnauds and Gordon take a train ride to Quedlinburg. During a stop in Neinstedt, Gordon again shows off his vast knowledge of

23. Chambers, *Supernatural and Irrational Elements,* 120.

the area and one of its well-known families. "Überhaupt sind die besten Geschichten uralt und überall zu Haus, also Welteigentum, und ich habe manche, von denen wir glaubten, daß sie zwischen Havell und Spree das Licht der Welt erblickten oder ohne die Gebrüder Grimm gar nicht existieren würden, in Tibet und am Himalaja wiedergefunden" (Overall, the best stories are very old and are at home everywhere, that is, they belong to the world. I have found some stories in Tibet and the Himalayas that we believed either first saw the light of day between the Havel and the Spree, or would not even exist without the brothers Grimm, C 173). Again, Gordon's remarks and his ensuing argument with another member of the party are ironically interrupted by the "abermalig" (repetitive) stopping of the train. His emphasis on old stories as a mode of explanation is again underscored by the literally repetitive nature of the train, and, as Downing points out, both old and new modes of explanation function as equally acceptable forms of reality. Everything in nature, including the train, becomes repeatable or exchangeable, and nothing lends itself to perfect mimetic representation.[24] Hence "the very old stories" become the railway, and the railway, logically, becomes its own type of old story through repetition.

The depiction of the dialectic of myth and enlightenment reaches a climax at the end of the twelfth and fifteenth chapters. In a manner that prefigures the character of Innstetten in *Effi Briest,* St. Arnaud scares Cécile with stories of trains and ghosts. In chapter 12, the others in their party have gone on, while the St. Arnauds, because Cécile has exhausted herself, rest on a bench. Cécile is relaxed and startled out of sweet dreams when "plötzlich an der Bahn entlang die Signale gezogen wurden und von Thale her das scharfe Läuten der Abfahrtsglocke herüberklang . . . so vernahm man auch schon den Pfiff der Lokomotive, gleich danach ein Keuchen und Prusten, und nun dampfte der

---

24. Downing, *Double Exposures,* 8–9.

Zug auf wenig hundert Schritt an dem Lindenberge vorüber" (suddenly along the rail, the signal sounded and from the valley the sharp sounds of departure bells rang ... one could already make out the whistle of the locomotive, and shortly thereafter a chugging and puffing. Then the train steamed by less than a hundred steps away from the Lindenberg, C 207). Upon noticing the train, St. Arnaud tells Cécile that it is destined for Berlin and, playing on her fear and weakened condition, asks sadistically if she would like to be on that train, to which Cécile replies, "Nein, nein" (C 207). Although the reader is not fully aware at this point of the significance of this question, the depiction of the train adds to the sense of foreboding caused by St. Arnaud's disingenuous inquiry. Fontane writes, "Nun sahen beide wieder der Wagenreihe nach und horchten auf das Echo, das das Gerassel und Geklapper in den Bergen wachrief und fast so klang, als ob immer neue Züge vom Hexentanzplatz her herunterkämen" (Now they watched the row of rail cars pass and listened to the echo that the rattling and clattering awakened in the mountains, almost as if ever more trains were coming down from the Place of the Witches' Dance, C 207). Inasmuch as the *Hexentanzplatz* is described earlier in the work as an area where witches are commonplace (C 165), Chambers is correct to conclude that the echo provides the train with a supernatural air.[25] The essence of the strange effect, a point she does not make, is the repetition inherent in the echo that seems to create the illusion of more and more trains coming out of this enchanted place. Through the myth of the *Hexentanzplatz* and its repetition, the villagers are able to assuage their fear of the unknown. This fear gives way to enlightenment, another means of understanding—hence the appearance of the train coming out of the *Hexentanzplatz*. In this passage the train is turned into myth by the echo, a myth in its own right dealing with another voiceless woman and unrequited love. This echo provides the train with its repetition, in this

---

25. Chambers, *Supernatural and Irrational Elements*, 106.

instance quite literally. The reader is not yet aware of the complete context of the fear, but the menacing mood created by this dialectic makes it all the more poignant.

At the end of chapter 15, the reader is confronted with much the same thing. This time, instead of the train appearing before the witches, St. Arnaud, in an arrogant and condescending manner, asks Cécile if she would like to take a walk to the *Hexentanzplatz*. "Siehe nur, wie das Mondlicht drüben auf die Felsen fällt. Alles Spukhaft; lauter groteske Leiber und Physiognomien . . . Herr von Gordon hatte recht, als er den ganzen Harz eine Hexengegend nannte" (Just look how the moonlight falls there on the cliffs. All is ghostly; lots of grotesque, shadowy bodies and forms. Mr. Gordon was right when he called the entire Harz mountains a witches' region, C 239). St. Arnaud, Cécile, and Gordon, all on horseback, are suddenly startled: "Unten im Tal von Quedlinburg und der Teufelsmauer her, kam im selben Augenblicke klappernd und rasselnd der letzte Zug heran, und das Mondlicht durchleuchtete die weiße Rauchwolke, während vorn zwei Feueraugen blitzten und die Funken der Maschine weit hin ins Feld flogen" (Down in the valley from Quedlinburg and the Devil's Wall, the last train came rattling and clattering by, and the moonlight shone through the white cloud of steam, while in front, two eyes of fire flashed and sparks from the machine flew far into the field, C 239). Although their surprise is provoked by the eerie atmosphere created by St. Arnaud, there is no denying that the train here, more so than in the previous passage, has taken on an aspect of the supernatural and the demonic that we have already seen in the works of Auerbach and Rosegger, as they depict how the generally uninformed perceive the train as a snorting monster delivered straight from hell. Heinimann explains this passage as signaling the possibility of a quick change between the idyll of the Harz and the city of Berlin.[26] This is perceptive, but I think Chambers is again closer

---

26. Heinimann, *Technische Innovation*, 238.

to the mark when she points out that the supernatural air of the train reflects the out-of-control forces at work here—though again she does not go far enough.[27] The supernatural as Chambers describes it is roughly equivalent to Adorno and Horkheimer's concept of myth, our attempt to gain control of seemingly uncontrollable and frightening forces. Because St. Arnaud has exacerbated Cécile's fear, the train in this passage is depicted as more demonic than is the train in chapter 12. Also, Cécile has greater reason to fear inasmuch as she finds herself falling in love with Gordon—thus risking the type of relationship that caused the social ostracism in the first place. In fact, Chambers sees the seemingly uncontrollable train as a metaphor for the confused, uncontrollable emotions shared by Cécile and Gordon.[28] Hence the familiar constellation of fear, repetition, myth, and enlightenment again appears in an artistic manner, only this time the fear is intensified, as is the mythical nature of the train.

The next time the train appears, it is associated with Gordon. He is a cable man and as such is called away on urgent business. His departure from Cécile is rushed; as he takes his leave of her, he waves goodbye through an opening in the high hedge that separates the park meadow from the train station. The spatial imagery is effective. On the one side is the reality of the train station—the end of the idyll—on the other is the apparent idyll in the park. Gordon stands in the middle, in an opening in the hedge that divides the two worlds. This is representative of Gordon in general; he is a combination of an aristocrat and a civil engineer who specializes in international cable-laying projects.[29] Thus he stands between the apparently idyllic life of the nobility and the hard reality of technological innovation as a democratizing agent, which threatens that idyllic life. In fact, it is one of these democratizers that removes him from his idyll. The inner monologue he carries on while riding the train

27. Chambers, *Supernatural and Irrational Elements*, 107.
28. Ibid.
29. Korte, *Ordnung und Tabu*, 108.

out of town reinforces his conflicted state of mind. He is haunted by the question of whether he should see Cécile again, with whether he should pursue her. Here again the train is juxtaposed with myth. As he sits in his backward-facing seat, he is flooded with memories of his time in Thale. The reader imagines these images passing by as if outside the window of the train, much like a film reel. When Gordon loses sight of the mountains (which include the enchanted *Roßtrappe* and *Hexentanzplatz*), he resolves that he should not pursue Cécile. Then, as the train makes a sharp turn, he changes his seat to regain the agreeable view. In his new seat, with a clearer view of this enchanted world, he questions his initial resolve and ultimately changes his mind, a decision that leads to his death in the duel with St. Arnaud.

St. Arnaud serves as Gordon's foil or, more accurately, as a foil to one aspect of Gordon's personality. This relationship echoes that between the Civil Servant and Heister in Auerbach's *Sträflinge,* between the Postmaster and Lechner in Rosegger's *Die neue Bahn,* and between Wieser and Yark in Rosegger's *Das ewige Licht.* Whereas Gordon, at least in one persona, is the worldly, well-traveled man of the new era, St. Arnaud is the old. St. Arnaud is himself almost the embodiment of a myth—the myth of what it is to be Prussian. He was wounded in battle at St. Denis in 1870 in the Franco-Prussian War—by a miracle shot that penetrated his neck but managed to go between his carotid artery and his windpipe. He was back on his feet in six weeks, and the story became legendary. St. Arnaud has also been known to race trains on horseback. When he fails to return from the duel with Gordon, Cécile thinks: "vielleicht [macht er] ein[en] Wettritt neben dem Eisenbahnzuge her" (maybe he's out racing against the train again, *C* 312). St. Arnaud also killed a man in a duel, presumably for Cécile's honor, but as we come to find out in his duel with Gordon, he is much less chivalrous than that. He fights both duels for his own empty sense of honor, a hollow, face-saving move that has nothing to do with selfless virtue and chivalry. He is truly associated with the old, but in St. Arnaud we see that the old is a chimera, and that he will have nothing to do with a new order. Nevertheless, through the repetition of his "heroic" deeds, he has become almost mythical.

Gordon, by contrast, is a man in transition. On one hand he is part of the new order; on the other he remains an aristocrat. He is by profession a communicator who, ironically, is undone by his inability to communicate. Not only is he a cable man; he served his military time as an engineer in a railway regiment, a marked contrast to St. Arnaud's service in the cavalry. In the end, however, he cannot overcome his narrow aristocratic persona. He presumes, much like the rest of polite society, that the rumors regarding Cécile's past life as the mistress to a prince must be true, and that she therefore does not deserve his homage but has earned his untoward attentions. Müller-Seidel correctly suggests that, when it comes to Cécile and his judgment about her, Gordon remains trapped by the contradictory mores of his social class.[30] In his lack of independence, he is much like General Saldern, whom we encountered in the opening chapter, and the rest of the aristocracy. It is ironic, however, that the early comment on independence is uttered by St. Arnaud, who is equally a slave to social convention and conformity. In fact, St. Arnaud's hypocrisy is one of the things that link him to Gordon. Müller-Seidel points out that after he learns of Gordon's actions, St. Arnaud is no less contradictory in his behavior than Gordon. St. Arnaud treats Cécile indifferently, and the fact that he risks his life in a duel is simply socially determined.[31] Echoing this sentiment, Hans-Heinrich Reuter suggests that Gordon, the apparently prejudice-free man of the world, takes the same typically masculine approach to Cécile that St. Arnaud does.[32] Hence Gordon never truly transcends his aristocratic side.

30. Müller-Seidel, *Theodor Fontane*, 193.
31. Ibid.
32. Hans-Heinrich Reuter, *Fontane* (Berlin: Verlag der Nation, 1995), 2:680.

The final word on myth versus enlightenment is literally the final word in the novel, and it is not explicitly related to the train. The work ends with a letter from Pastor Dörffel to St. Arnaud, advising him of the circumstances of Cécile's untimely death. The letter ends with the biblical passage, "Der Friede Gottes . . . der über alle Vernunft ist, sei mit uns allen" (The peace of God . . . which is above all reason, be with us all, *C* 317). Myth is given supremacy over reason—though it would be simplistic to say that since St. Arnaud kills Gordon, myth "kills" reason. The biblical passage does not recognize the myth inherent in reason or, for that matter, inherent in enlightenment. St. Arnaud repeats his duel and continues as the living embodiment of myth, but enlightenment also repeats, for it is the train as the embodiment of reason and enlightenment that repeats as well. Both combatants travel by train to the duel; both leave by train as well. Gordon's corpse travels on a funeral train to Liegnitz, while St. Arnaud makes his escape on a train from Sachsen to the Riviera.

Effi Briest

Fontane took up the themes of marital infidelity and honor as exemplified by the duel eight years later in what is perhaps his best known work, *Effi Briest*. At seventeen, Effi is forced, largely owing to social convention, to marry her mother's former suitor, Geerd von Instetten, a man more than twice her age. She moves out of her father's home and into the cold, isolated, and frightening abode of Instetten in the northern German town of Kessin. After some time, and for many reasons, Effi has an affair with Major Crampas, a womanizing acquaintance of Instetten. Shortly after the affair, she and Instetten move to Berlin. Several years later, while Effi is away taking a cure, Instetten discovers damning evidence of Effi's affair with Crampas in the form of their letters. She is shunned from this point by her own daughter and ostracized by her parents and society in general, thanks, ironically, to the same social convention that dictated that she marry at age seventeen. Instetten promptly, but not without reservations, challenges Effi's former lover to a duel and kills him. After years of isolation, Effi, who is now chronically ill, is invited by her parents to return home and live out her remaining days with them in Hohen-Cremmin, where she eventually dies.

The most relevant aspects of *Effi Briest* for my purposes are the two mentioned most often—the Chinese ghost and the train. Of the latter, Heinimann suggests that the function of the railway in this work is much less significant than it is in *Cécile*. We must presume he means that the train is not as significant, thematically speaking, for if the train were measured by the number of times it makes an appearance in *Effi Briest,* he would have to conclude just the opposite. Heinimann acknowledges that there is more rail travel in *Effi Briest* than in *Cécile*.[33] Both of his statements about the significance and the number of occurrences of the train, however, are simplistic and not wholly relevant. Inasmuch as the railway plays almost exactly the same role in both works, the train in *Effi Briest* holds just as much relative importance as it does in *Cécile*. It is one key to understanding the novel as a whole.

Thematically, Heinimann suggests (as he does with regard to *Cécile)* that the rail in *Effi Briest* generally represents escape from a restrictive, husband-dominated relationship.[34] While this is true to some extent, Segeberg's analysis is more specific and compelling. He suggests that Fontane does not employ technological means as mere social artifacts but uses them in a more calculated way, most often to reflect fear or happiness. Segeberg compares trains and other technological innovations to Innstetten's ghost, which he claims Instetten invented solely as a means of punish-

---

33. Heinimann, *Technische Innovation,* 241.
34. Ibid., 242.

ing his young wife.³⁵ Although the reason for Instetten's invention of the ghost may be overstated here, he is certainly correct in his comparison of the ghost and technology. They do, in some instances, serve the same purpose, and, as in *Cécile,* this certainly suggests an understanding of the relationship between the technological and the mythological in Fontane, whether conscious or unconscious.

A brief look at the reception of the ghost by literary critics may be useful. Over the decades that have passed since the publication of *Effi Briest,* a great deal has been written about the Chinese ghost. As I mentioned in the Introduction, the mid-twentieth-century critic J. P. Stern echoed a prevailing view of the ghost when he referred to it as the "only blemish" in the work and "a piece of bric-a-brac left over by poetic realism."³⁶ Modern critics like Richard Brinkmann, Erika Swales, and Helen Chambers began to align themselves more often with Fontane himself, who, in a letter to Josef Widmann, wrote of the ghost, "Sie sind der erste, der auf das Spukhaus und den Chinesen hinweist; ich begreife nicht, wie man daran vorbeisehen kann, denn erstlich ist dieser Spuk, so bilde ich mir wenigstens ein, an und für sich interessant, und zweitens, wie Sie hervorgehoben haben, steht die Sache nicht zum Spaß da, sondern ist ein Drehpunkt für die ganze Geschichte" (You are the first to allude to the haunted house and the Chinese ghost; I don't understand how people can overlook that because first, the ghost, at least as I imagine it, is interesting in and of itself, and second, as you suggest, the ghost is not there for fun, rather it is a turning point for the entire story)—thus assigning the ghost a much more critical role than Stern grants it.³⁷

---

35. Segeberg, *Literatur im technischen Zeitalter,* 177.
36. Stern, *"Effi Briest, Madame Bovary, Anna Karenina,"* 374.
37. Theodor Fontane, "An Josef Victor Widmann," 19 Nov. 1895, in *In Freiheit dienen: Briefe von Theodor Fontane,* ed. Friedrich Seebaß (Munich: Hanser, 1956), 107. For further discussion on this most critical aspect of *Effi Briest,* see Richard Brinkmann, *Theodor Fontane: Über die Verbindlichkeit des*

While she may not exactly conceive of the ghost as a turning point in this work, Chambers does point out the complex nature of the ghost motif. First, she argues that the ghost is "an indispensable element in the underlying structure of the novel . . . use[d] not only to symbolise and suggest flaws in the marital relationship, but also to chart the development and deterioration of that relationship."[38] The train serves this purpose as well. For example, the honeymoon train ride to Italy, which gives Instetten an opportunity to teach Effi about the wider world, provides the soil for the seed Crampas later plants in Effi's mind regarding Instetten. She tells Crampas of Instetten's ghost stories and he suggests that Instetten operates "erzieherisch, [er] ist der geborene Pädagog" (didactically, [he] is a born teacher, *EB* 133).[39] This comment immediately begins to gnaw at Effi and creates just enough of a rift in her marriage for Crampas to exploit in making his own advances.

Later in the novel, two scenes involving the train mark the end of their relationship. Regarding her affair, Effi concludes, "Aber Scham über meine Schuld, die hab ich nicht oder doch nicht so recht oder doch nicht genug, und das bringt mich um, daß ich sie nicht habe . . . etwas [ist] nicht in Ordnung in meiner Seele" (But I don't feel any shame over my guilt, I don't feel any real shame, or rather not enough, and it is killing me that I have no shame . . . something [is] amiss in my soul, *EB* 219). After reaching this conclusion, a train appears, becomes louder, and finally fades and dies out—a parallel to her marriage to Instetten. Shortly thereafter Instetten considers his own actions.

Unverbindlichen (Munich: Piper, 1967); Peter Demetz, *Formen des Realismus: Theodor Fontane, Kritische Untersuchungen* (Munich: Hanser, 1964); Charlotte Jolles, *Theodor Fontane* (Stuttgart: Metzler, 1993); Müller-Seidel, *Theodor Fontane;* Reuter, *Fontane;* Frances M. Subiotto, "The Ghost in *Effi Briest*," *Forum for Modern Language Studies* 21, no. 2 (1985): 137–50.

38. Chambers, *Supernatural and Irrational Elements,* 209.

39. All *Effi Briest* excerpts are from *Romane, Erzählungen, Gedichte,* sec. 1, vol. 4 of *Sämtliche Werke,* ed. Walter Keitel (Munich: Hanser, 1963), 7–296.

He continues to struggle with questions of honor, justice, and limitations when he determines that it is all a comedy, and he concludes that he must maintain the comedy. "[Er] muß Effi wegschicken und sie ruinieren und [sich] mit" ([He] must send Effi away and ruin her along with [himself], *EB* 243), thus marking the official end of the marriage. Hence the train, like the ghost, is an effective gauge of Effi and Instetten's marriage.

Chambers also argues that manifestations like the ghost are not necessarily the cause of fear but rather a reflection of the fear of the inevitability of events that is actually caused by a dangerous mix of irrational, uncontrollable powers in the personalities of the principals and in upper-class society.[40] This, too, is remarkably similar to the function of the railway in this work. What better symbol of inevitability than the train that keeps coming around the clock, day in and day out, regardless of circumstances? In addition to the unavoidability of the train, it is also often associated with those very same unbiddable forces in the characters and their society. Effi's desire to remain a child, Instetten's need to control Effi as a father would control his daughter, and the requirements of nineteenth-century German society's code of honor are all examples of these forces. That the ghost and the railway play such similar roles in this work provides further evidence of the close relationship between myth and enlightenment, which both serve as a means of conquering fear and uncertainty.

This point culminates in the pivotal sleigh-ride scene. As Heinimann points out, this scene is central to our understanding of Fontane's use of the train, but Heinimann fails to highlight a vital aspect of this passage. He does not make the connection between the end of the scene, when the characters arrive at the train station, and the beginning of the scene, which includes the most thorough discussion of the ghost. In this passage, both

---

40. Chambers, *Supernatural and Irrational Elements*, 120.

the train and the ghost are, as Segeberg suggests with regard to technology in Fontane's works, calculated apparatuses of fear.[41]

The scene begins as Effi and Instetten discuss how they will spend their day. Instetten suggests a sleigh ride to the train station and lunch at the Zum Fürsten Bismarck (Prince Bismarck). On the way to the train station, the pair pass a cemetery, and Instetten points out that the Chinese man, the one who haunts Effi now, is buried there. Effi's fear is immediate and palpable: "Effi fuhr zusammen: es war ihr wie ein Stich. Aber sie hatte doch Kraft genug, sich zu beherrschen, und fragte mit anscheinender Ruhe: 'Unserer?'" (Effi started: it was like a stab. But she had enough strength to get control of herself and asked with apparent calm: 'Ours?'" *EB* 83). Tired of her own fear, Effi insists in so many words that Instetten disenchant this whole prospect of the ghost. She begs, "Erzähle mir das Wirkliche. Die Wirklichkeit kann mich nicht so quälen wie meine Phantasie" (Tell me about something real. Reality cannot possibly torment me as much as my imagination, *EB* 84). In this way she differentiates herself from Cécile, who asks St. Arnaud for a story about happiness and joy. Cécile is asking for a fairytale, while Effi begs for reality. Effi is a stronger person than Cécile, but she does not realize that reality in the form of the train will soon torment her in much the same way that the ghost has.

Instetten relates the factual history of the Chinese man who becomes the ghost, but he does not seem to want to disenchant entirely. In the middle of his history, he sees the church tower before them. He suggests that they give up the train station, give up this search for the presumed comfort of reality that Effi desires, in favor of the church, in favor of myth. Effi rejects the idea, and they continue to the train station, Instetten explaining all the while the history of the ghost. But Effi is not consoled even by the time they reach the train station.

While at the station, the arrival of a train provides another

---

41. Segeberg, *Literatur im technischen Zeitalter*, 177.

opportunity for Instetten to torture Effi emotionally. Just as the "reality" of the history of the Chinese man never truly comforts her, neither does this manifestation of reality, the train, but much the reverse. As Instetten teases Effi with the suggestion of going home to Hohen-Cremmin, "Effi war, als der Zug vorbeijagte, von einer herzlichen Sehnsucht erfaßt worden. So gut es ihr ging, sie fühlte sich trotzdem wie in einer fremden Welt" (As the train raced by, Effi was gripped by a heartfelt longing. As well as she was doing, she felt as if she were in a strange world, *EB* 89). Thanks to the train, she feels a longing for her lost childhood combined with a fear of the strange new world into which she has entered. Hence the literary devices of the train and the ghost play largely the same role. In this case, both myth and technology serve to intensify Effi's fear.

The final scene to deal with the train takes place when Effi has finally been welcomed back into her parents' home. She is very ill, and her only pleasures are her dog Rollo and taking walks along the paved road that leads to the train station. As she walks, she hears the oncoming train, closes her eyes, and gives herself over to sweet forgetfulness. Heinimann correctly points out that the reader is immediately reminded of the end of the sleigh-ride scene; it is similar in that both journeys have the train station as their goal.[42] The differences, however, are important. Gone is the ghost, and gone are the fear and longing. The train is no longer juxtaposed with the ghost, or with Instetten, for that matter; it also no longer acts as a reflection of Effi's fear. Effi has traveled a great distance, both literally and figuratively, from that scene that took place so early in her marriage.

The passage continues: "In Nähe der Station, hart an der Chaussee, lag eine Chausseewalze. Das war ihr täglicher Rastplatz, von dem aus [Effi] das Treiben auf dem Bahndamm verfolgen konnte; Züge kamen und gingen, und mitunter sah sie zwei Rauchfahnen, die sich einen Augenblick wie deckten und dann

---

42. Heinimann, *Technische Innovation*, 243.

nach links und rechts hin wieder auseinandergingen, bis sie hinter Dorf und Wäldchen verschwanden" (Near the station, right next to the avenue, was a bench. This was her daily resting place, from which she could observe the doings on the rail embankment; trains came and went, and now and then she saw two columns of smoke, which at first appeared as one and then split left and right until they disappeared behind the village and the forest, *EB* 290–91). This is another transfiguring moment that occurs in light of the train. The transfiguration does not, in this instance, lead Effi to remorse, as in the sleigh-ride scene. Although they have been interpreted as representative of Effi and Crampas, the pillars of smoke are more representative of Effi and Instetten.[43] The image is presented not in the spirit of spite or regret but rather that of "süßes Vergessen" (sweet forgetting, *EB* 291)—a final reflection of the state of Effi's relationship with Instetten. Effi has come to terms with her past, and this, as Heinimann quite rightly points out, is the only time that the train takes on a positive meaning for her.[44]

Fontane's works seem to provide further evidence that despair over the demise of the old metaphysic is unwarranted. His art, as Erika Swales suggests, "betrays the consciousness of its time, betrays it in both senses of the word; it bears the imprint of its time, it renders details of the physical and psychological landscape of the society it evokes . . . but it also betrays its time by transgressing the given consciousness of which it partakes."[45] Thus the ghost as the transgressor of the given time and the train as part of the physical and psychological landscape of the nineteenth century can exist in the same work. As Alan Bance says, Fontane "presents a world which is only apparently *entzaubert* (emptied of magic), and in *Effi Briest* he retains the pre-scientific power of magic to which we are all still subject, how-

---

43. Williams, *Monster in the Mirror,* 253.
44. Heinimann, *Technische Innovation,* 243.
45. Erika Swales, "Private Mythologies and Public Unease: On Fontane's *Effi Briest," Modern Language Review* 75 (1980): 123–24.

ever rational we like to think ourselves."[46] Bance is right about this, but he does not go far enough. What Adorno and Horkheimer suggest is that the prescientific power of magic and the power of science have the same roots. Thus when Bance refers to Fontane as an "exploiter of transitional moments for fictional ends,"[47] he overstates how great the leap must be to make the transition. Bance and others do not consider the resilience of repetition, the shared root of science and myth, as a means of explanation. Through repetition, humans have a remarkable capacity to incorporate a new tale into older ones that have been told for thousands of years. It is not necessary to invent a story for a new age out of nothing. Writers like Auerbach, Rosegger, and Fontane do not invent. Through their repeated juxtaposition of rail and fairytale, myth and enlightenment, they highlight the resilient shared root of both realms. This is precisely what we shall see in the two works by Gerhart Hauptmann discussed in the next chapter.

46. Alan Bance, *Theodor Fontane: The Major Novels* (Cambridge: Cambridge University Press, 1982), 55.
47. Alan Bance, "Fontane and the Notion of Progress," *Publications of the English Goethe Society* 57 (1988): 11.

[5]

GERHART HAUPTMANN

So erklärte [Thiel] sein Wärterhäuschen und die Bahnstrecke, die er zu besorgen hatte, insgeheim gleichsam für geheiligtes Land, welches ausschließlich den Manen der Toten gewidmet sein sollte.

Thus [Thiel] secretly declared his rail house and the stretch of rail he maintained as sacred land, which is to be dedicated solely to the worship of the dead.

Gerhart Hauptmann, Bahnwärter Thiel (The Linesman Thiel) (1888)

Gerhart Hauptmann was born in Obersalzbrunn in Silesia in 1862, more than twenty-five years after the first railway in Germany was built. By the time of Hauptmann's birth the system was flourishing, with approximately 12,150 kilometers of rail lines, more than half of them in Prussia.[1] In his notes to an edition of Hauptmann's *Bahnwärter Thiel,* Klaus Post discusses the rather interesting role the railway played in the life of the young Hauptmann. Early in his life, Hauptmann's parents owned a hotel in Salzbrunn, *Zur Preußischen Krone* (the Prussian Crown). When Hauptmann was seventeen years old, his father was forced to sell the operation owing to financial difficulties stemming

---

1. Fremdling "Industrialisierung und Eisenbahn," 131.

from two economic crises and a boycott of sorts by eastern European guests after the unification of Germany in 1871. In order to earn a living, his father bought a restaurant on the railway in the town of Sorgau.² As his parents were busy with the management of this new enterprise, young Hauptmann often found himself alone or in the company of people associated with the rail in one way or another.³

Post suggests that these events had a purely negative impact on the young Hauptmann. Neglected by his mother, he began to see the locomotive and the rails as a symbol of the future, not as a repetition of mythical ur-images but as an expression of the spirit of the era. "Hauptmann mußte erschrecken vor den Zeichen dieser Kultur," writes Post. "Nicht deshalb, weil er den Fortschritt verabscheute, sondern weil er feinfühlig erspürte, daß der Fortschritt erkauft wurde durch den Verlust elementarster menschlicher Bindungen" (Hauptmann had to be frightened by the signs of this culture. Not because he loathed progress, but because intuitively he sensed that progress was purchased at the cost of the most basic human relationships).⁴ Post sees Hauptmann as similar to those who, like Rudolf Eucken, maintained that progress was bought with the soul of humankind.⁵ Whether Post is right or not, the move from Salzbrunn to Sorgau and the decline in status that accompanied the loss of the hotel became for the young Hauptmann inextricably linked to the spirit of progress, described by Camphausen as "das Streben aller Völker nach materiellem Wohl" (the striving of all peoples after material well-being),⁶ that dominated the late nineteenth century. But it is a bit of a Freudian overstatement to claim, as Post does, that *Bahnwärter Thiel* is Hauptmann's elegiac lament, his poetic illus-

---

2. Klaus D. Post, "Afterword" to *Bahnwärter Thiel,* by Gerhart Hauptmann (Munich: Hanser, 1979), 95–97.
3. Warren R. Maurer, *Gerhart Hauptmann* (Boston: Twayne, 1982), 5.
4. Post, "Afterword," 97.
5. Eucken, "Innere Mensch," 33.
6. Quoted in Schwann, *Ludwig Camphausen,* 288.

tration of two difficulties. Post claims that *Bahnwärter Thiel* expresses Hauptmann's loss of connection to his mother. He also maintains that the novella depicts the spiritual world, represented by a technological innovation, gone awry and turned against humankind.[7] Despite this overblown rhetoric, it is certain that the railway had a tremendous impact on Hauptmann's early childhood memories, which probably affected his approach to the railway and other instruments of progress.

A passage from *Das Abenteuer meiner Jugend (The Adventure of My Youth)* (1937), raises doubts that Hauptmann's youthful experiences with the railway and progress in general were as negative as Post suggests. As this essay contains his only substantive nonfictional statement on the railway, it is worth quoting in its entirety:

Die Züge donnerten aus der Ferne davon. Die Mauern erbebten, die Wartesäle erzitterten. Diese Geräusche gingen ins Blut, diese Bewegungen waren Kraftquellen. Leisetreterische Schwäche, selbstische Tatenlosigkeit, verbunden mit kopfhängerischem religiösen Grillenfang, wurden hier zur Erbärmlichkeit. Hier war der Geist einer kommenden Zeit, die mit Weltuntergang und ähnlichem Unsinn nicht rechnete. Diese Maschinen, die in unermüdlichen Eifer mit gleichsam heiter wehenden Rauchfahnen kamen und gingen, die stolz und froh ihre Pflicht taten, die rannten und rannten, Entfernungen zwischen Menschen zunichte machend, würden vor keinem Faulpelz haltmachen. Sie würden ihn kurz und klein hacken... wenn [er] nicht aus dem Wege [ging], zu Mus machen. Dem Mütigen war die Welt eine einizige Herrlichkeit. Der aber gehörte nicht hinein, der darauf bestünde, ihm müßten die gebratenen Tauben ins Maul fliegen.

From afar, the trains thundered away. The walls quaked, the waiting rooms shook. These noises became a part of you, these movements were sources of strength. Pussyfooting weakness, selfish idleness coupled with a head-hanging religious pessimism, turned to wretchedness. This was the spirit of a nascent era that took no account of concepts like the end of the world and other such nonsense. These machines, in

---

7. Post "Afterword," 97–98.

tireless enthusiasm, with cheerfully blowing columns of smoke, came and went. These machines that did their duty happily and proudly, that ran and ran, eating up distances between people, would not stop for any lazybones. The trains would hack him into tiny pieces . . . if the lazybones did not get out of the way . . . turn [him] into mush. To the brave, the world was a singular splendor. He who insisted that the world owes him a living, however, does not belong to this new era.[8]

These hardly seem the words of a man whose psyche suffered permanent damage at the hands of the relentless forces of progress, as Post argues. When Hauptmann refers to the movement of the trains as sources of power that have nothing to do with the end of the world, and when he points out all of the virtues of the railway, he sounds very much like that unabashed enthusiast of progress, Berthold Auerbach. Hauptmann seems to reject the images of decay and destruction wrought by the railway that Rosegger ultimately portrayed in *Das ewige Licht*. But in none of Hauptmann's works of fiction is there any enthusiasm for technological advances, and thus we cannot presume that this passage from *Das Abenteuer meiner Jugend* conveys his ultimate view of the matter. The fact is that Hauptmann, like Rosegger, is deeply conflicted on the question of technology. On the one hand there is this clear expression of enthusiasm for technology, while on the other are the fictional testimonies of *Bahnwärter Thiel* and of one of Hauptmann's best-known dramas, *Die Weber (The Weavers)* (1892), in which the new technology is clearly associated, if not with the "end of the world," then with its generally negative impact on society and the individual.

Hauptmann, Realism, and Mythology

Hauptmann's ambivalence emerges in two works penned in 1888: a poem entitled "Im Nachtzug" ("In the Night Train") and

8. Gerhart Hauptmann, *Das Abenteuer meiner Jugend,* in *Sämtliche Werke,* comp. Hans-Egon Hass (Berlin: Propyläen, 1962), 7:760–61.

his famous novella *Bahnwärter Thiel*. His approach to the railway in these works is as interesting as it is complex. The rail is not as simplistic as the metropolitan railway in Max Kretzer's *Meister Timpe (Master Timpe)* (1888). In this novel, which appeared in the same year as Hauptmann's two 1888 works, the construction of the metropolitan railway in Berlin and its ultimate completion is primarily a symbol of the inevitability of the coming industrial age—a destroyer of the old and a harbinger of the new. Hauptmann's works are more complicated, for he mythologizes, Christianizes, and (one might say) naturalizes the railway to such a degree that the reader cannot tell whether the "end of the world" is a merely technological affair or whether it suggests a larger, more comprehensive narrative that includes both myth and science.

It is perhaps more awkward to be discussing myth in the case of a naturalist like Hauptmann than it was in the case of Fontane. Naturalists, after all, supposedly deal in a version of reality that is bare and unaestheticized. They are the artists who attempt to represent the world exactly as it is, unadorned, free of mythological trappings. In their zest for exact reproduction, they are, to use a term coined by Robert Holub, nothing more than "super realists." They fall into the same trap as the realists, that is, of striving for some kind of "pure" mimesis that is by definition unattainable. Holub says that naturalism is nothing more than the "culmination of the realist epoch."[9] Hauptmann, too, spent his life fighting against the "naturalist" label because he was so taken aback by the "ultimately dehumanizing implications" of that movement.[10] For one thing, mythology was too important in his view for him to embrace naturalism uncritically. Post argues that myth had a very specific function for Hauptmann: it allowed him to express things that mere language could not.

---

9. Holub, *Reflections of Realism*, 203.
10. Warren R. Maurer, *Understanding Gerhart Hauptmann* (Columbia: University of South Carolina Press, 1992), 17.

Hauptmann, according to Post, found words an inadequate means for the expression of the ineffable mystery of existence. For Hauptmann, myth was the most effective means of expressing the human condition. Thiel, in Post's view, was destroyed not because of a society that oppressed him but because he was under the control of irrational forces—the chthonian love of Lene and the mystically demetric motherly love of Minna.[11] Maurer concurs: "Unconvincing Marxist interpretations to the contrary, the causes of the Thiel family tragedy derive more directly from universal human circumstances than from socioeconomic problems."[12] Thus the naturalist aspects of this work, as well as those of "Im Nachtzug," are subdued, and both works defy easy categorization.

Post is correct, for in these two works mythological narrative serves as more than mere background; it is the catalyst that drives the action in *Bahnwärter Thiel* and the provocation behind the narrator's thoughts in "Im Nachtzug." Both counter Mahr's point that nineteenth-century authors faced irresolvable conflicts when they tried to depict new technological innovations within the context of old constructs of imagination and the language of the past.[13] If Mahr were correct, then Hauptmann, as a naturalist, was supposed to have abandoned the magical springtime and enchanted highlands of his poem and the eerie pine forest of his novella, but to abandon these was to abandon the old constructs, the familiar narrative. Despite my rejection of his claims, this dissonance to which Mahr so often refers did inspire these two noteworthy works of nineteenth-century literature.

11. Post, "Afterword," 119.
12. Maurer, *Gerhart Hauptmann*, 127.
13. Mahr, *Eisenbahnen in der deutschen Dichtung*, 160.

"Im Nachtzug"

In "Im Nachtzug" (see Appendix A),[14] the reader encounters a poet-traveler on a night train bound for an unknown destination. As this traveler sits in his seat among seven snoring companions, he contemplates, to the point of tears, the losses confronting modern technological man. He longs for the old concept of nature, with all its wonders and mysteries—elves and elfin maids and beautiful music—all of which humankind seems well on the way to explaining away with its new scientific narrative. The traveler's longing is jarringly interrupted by a new narrative that sings the praises not of magic or myth but rather of technology. A demon tells this story, advising the poet-traveler to listen to the rattling of the rails and not the sleepy, flirting marsh (lines 81–83). Despite the force of the demon's message, the music of old, the old mythological narrative, manages to surface one more time in its earth-transfiguring beauty (line 100), only to be scattered and drowned out by the tumultuous sounds of the train, leaving the poet-traveler with a burning longing for the engaging story of human existence as it was once told (lines 105–10).

This poem is more complex than it first appears. It seems at a glance to be saying that since the song of tumult, the new song of the nineteenth century, has the last word, it has won out. Mahr agrees with this surface interpretation. He believes that this poem registers the idea that the "Heide" (moor) in its natural/mystical form is no longer accessible to artists. Given the impact of the industrial age, it has lost its voice and cannot reach the poet. It is accessible only in dreams.[15] This interpretation, while interesting, is not entirely accurate. The moor as represen-

---

14. Gerhart Hauptmann, "Im Nachtzug," in *Ausgewählte Werke*, comp. Josef Gregor (Gütersloh: C. Bertelsmann Verlag, 1954), 5:12–14.
15. Mahr, *Eisenbahnen in der deutschen Dichtung*, 160.

tative of a mythological narrative is not inaccessible, nor has its voice completely disappeared. A closer analysis of the structure and content of the poem will help us to elucidate this point.

The form of "Im Nachtzug" is clearly nothing new. Hauptmann breaks no ground that would parallel the ascendancy of the technological era. The meter is a very consistent mix of iambic and dactylic, providing for a regular rhythm and giving the reader a sense of the steady rocking of the train. The same applies to the rhyme scheme. Each ten-line stanza begins with a four-line crossed rhyme, is followed by a rhymed couplet, and then closes with an enveloping rhyme. The regularity of the form seems to support Mahr's interpretation regarding the accessibility of the "moor," in that it gives the reader a sense of inevitability with regard to the train and technological advancement. But it may also be that, as with Rosegger's *Das ewige Licht*, the train has a soporific effect that dulls one's senses as to its true significance.

The sense of technological inevitability fades somewhat when one takes a closer look at the imagery of the poem. On one hand, Hauptmann presents the reader with the "Mondscheinreich" (empire of moonshine, line 21). In this empire, described in the third and fourth stanzas, magic reigns—the "Zauber der Nacht" (magic of the night, line 24) is underscored by the "zaubrische[en] und rein[en]" (magical and pure, line 40) musical sounds of the night. Further, this magical music is played by an elf (line 30), who entertains the personified "Gräslein" (blades of grass), "Rotklee" (red clover), "Maiblume" (mayflower), and "Au" (mead) (lines 30–36). Hauptmann employs much of the same personified nature imagery, though in a decidedly more positive tone, that Goethe does in his "Erlkönig" (The Erl-king) (1780). Hauptmann's imagery is from the old world, the world of Germanic and classical mythology, of the romantics and the pantheists, and certainly not of the nineteenth-century empiricists who relied primarily on a scientific narrative to explain the world.

The imagery of the empiricists, on closer analysis, however, is not so different from that of the magical Heide (moor). The empirical world of the train and the telegraph, in the narrator's words, cuts through the longing of the poet-traveler (lines 21–22). It is so powerful, in fact, that one would expect Hauptmann to employ some boldly unique imagery to describe this brave new world. He does not. He draws on the same stock of metaphor, image, and symbol that he used for the "Mondscheinreich" (empire of moonshine). Instead of musical elves, there is a threatening, evil presence who "aus dem Chaos [kommt mit] ein[em] Donnergesang, / zum Grauen zugleich und Erbarmen" (out of Chaos comes with a thundering song, / in horror as well as in mercy, lines 59–60). And Chaos is not the only classical image. The train is also propelled forward in its journey by "Zyklopen" (Cyclops, line 56). The evil presence of Chaos wants to shatter the chains (line 67)—a reference to Prometheus, provider of technology as symbolized by fire and man's greatest advocate to the gods.

Chaos, the void from which sprang earth (Gaia), night, day, and, in some traditions, love, is the ultimate myth of origin, according to Michael Grant and John Hazel in *Who's Who in Classical Mythology*.[16] It seems that Hauptmann either chose his mythological reference inappropriately—a highly unlikely proposition given his lifelong interest in mythology and his work late in life on modernizing Hellenic myth[17]—or his message is not simply that technology wins out over mythology. His point could be that technology shares the same origins as all other things human and all other things natural. There would then be no necessary conflict between technology and the old mythological narratives.

The same can be said of his portrayal of the Cyclops. In

---

16. Grant and Hazel, *Who's Who in Classical Mythology*, 83.
17. Robin A. Clouser, "The Spiritual Malaise of a Modern Hercules, Hauptmann's *Bahnwärter Thiel*," *Germanic Review* 50 (1980): 98.

Greek mythology, the three Cyclops sprang forth from Gaia after their father, Uranus, who feared them greatly, attempted to push them back into Gaia's womb.[18] This is yet another clever reference and it makes a nice parallel to rail technology. The pre-nineteenth-century thinkers who dwelled on the limitations of time and space[19] were the figurative fathers of this time-and-space-conquering technology. The inheritors of this line of thinking, the technological naysayers, seem to be playing the role of Uranus in their desire to push technology back into the Chaos whence it sprang. The problem with this, however, is evident in Hauptmann's third classical image. He makes a parallel between the advent of rail technology and the shattering of Prometheus's chains. The creation of the railway is placed on a par here with the acquisition of fire—a reference to the ambivalent reception of technological progress and the impossibility of "unthinking" something once it has been thought.

In addition, the demon is a pragmatist; he does not waste his time playing beautiful music like his elfin counterpart. He advises the poet-traveler that, "weil [du] den Elfen bewunder[st], / so sängen wir dir mit Donnergetön / das Lied so finster und doch so schön, / das Lied von unserem Jahrhundert!" (because [you] admire the elf, / we would sing to you the thundering tone / the song so dark and yet so beautiful, / the song of our century! lines 77–80). He explains that although he is a tough master who thirsts after blood and iron from his inventors, he can also be of assistance to the poor, presumably because they could improve their economic and social lot through him. This is another allusion to the dual nature of this momentous invention. It is both black devil and iron angel; dark yet beautiful; at once productive and destructive. The question remains: Is it ultimately destructive of an older mythological narrative?

---

18. Grant and Hazel, *Who's Who in Classical Mythology*, 96.
19. Lessing comes to mind here—*Hamburgische Dramaturgie* (1767), and the musings of the artist Conti in Lessing's masterpiece *Emilia Galotti* (1772).

In "Im Nachtzug," the old narrative gets one more chance. In the first six lines of the tenth stanza, Hauptmann hearkens back to the first stanza. We see again the poet-traveler keeping watch among the seven snoring noses, when slowly, out of the chaos and tumult, the old myth arises—in Hauptmann's words, effervesces—one more time. Only this time the tale is not classical but Christian. When the old tale finally breaks through, it sounds like a hymn, and not just any old hymn but a hymn of transfiguring beauty, which in the Christian faith is a story of the redemptive, forgiving nature of faith in God.

In the New Testament, both Mark and Luke write of the transfiguration. In Mark 9:2, Jesus takes Peter, James, and John "up on a mountain apart by themselves; and he [is] transfigured before them, and his garments [become] glistening, intensely white, as no fuller on earth could bleach them." Inasmuch as none of the disciples were present at Jesus' baptism, when he was proclaimed to be the son of God, this is a story of the inadequate faith of the disciples.[20] It took the transfiguration to make them understand Jesus' role on earth and to solidify their faith. Hauptmann's reference is probably an admonition to those not already blinded by technology to keep the faith. Hauptmann seems to be saying, "Just as Christ died and rose again, the old mythological narrative, despite being drowned out by technology, will rise again." Mark strengthens this interpretation in the remainder of his ninth book. After the transfiguration, Jesus goes on to exorcise a demon from the young son of a faithless father. So Hauptmann's technological demon has a Christian origin as well. For the faithful, the demigod of the railway will reign until the return of the old myth. In this sense "Im Nachtzug" is no farewell to the nonscientific, mythological narrative but quite the opposite.

This is precisely where Mahr errs. To presume that technol-

---

20. Raymond E. Brown, *An Introduction to the New Testament* (New York: Doubleday, 1997), 139.

ogy has displaced earlier versions of myth is to presume that it has prevailed in a power struggle over not just classical but also Christian myth. It is to presume that the narrative of science wins out over the mythological narrative. Despite what Mahr says, the moor as representative of earlier metaphysical thought is still accessible and still has its voice. The dissonance is not as irresolvable as Mahr would have it.[21] Perhaps the point is simply that the means of access are going to change, but the power of the myth and its associated imagery remains, if not on the surface then just under it, waiting to rise again with the creation of its own new myth or, more probably, an expansion of the old one. Whether this can happen only in dreams is also debatable, just as it always has been. Not everyone believed that Christ rose from the dead on the third day. Nor did the father believe the son that the way home was fraught with danger created by the elfin king in Goethe's "Erlkönig." Nor is it clear whether Coppola and Coppelius are one and the same in Hoffmann's *Der Sandmann (The Sandman)* (1817). The examples are endless; nothing has changed. Is the sound of the train simply that, a sound, or is it the music of Chaos? Is the moor simply that, or is it the dance floor for the elfin maid? Hauptmann shows in the imagery of "Im Nachtzug," whether this was his conscious intention or not, that the railway fits into the old mythological narrative very nicely. It simply extends the old in a way that helps us come to terms with the inherently frightening nature of the new. To recall Camphausen, perhaps Hauptmann shows that material well-being will not necessarily be the dominant drive of the age, that it will, of necessity, be subsumed under the larger heading of religion and politics, or myth and the application of power. It is also possible that the metaphysical vacuum feared by many thinkers of the time was merely a straw man.

---

21. See Mahr, *Eisenbahnen in der deutschen Dichtung,* 160.

Bahnwärter Thiel

The same straw man rears its head in *Bahnwärter Thiel*. Hauptmann's most famous novella tells the story of a simple railway linesman, Herculean in form and warmly disposed to his fellow man, who becomes so psychologically unhinged that he murders his wife and infant child. How and why he sinks to such a depth is the subject of this tightly structured "novellistische Studie." *Bahnwärter Thiel* is a "study" inasmuch as it is a psychological analysis of a single man. It is not a study of social and economic conditions, and in this sense it represents another departure by Hauptmann from the naturalist movement with which he is so closely associated in the latter half of the nineteenth century. It is not a radical departure in terms of the "milieu depicted; [the] attention to details of heredity; [the] undisguised emphasis on sexuality . . . [the] minutely detailed narrative style," among other things, but it is a departure nonetheless.[22]

Franz Thiel is a poor railway linesman whose first wife, Minna, a weak and sickly woman whom he loves dearly, dies in childbirth. The child, Tobias, survives and has the same weak disposition, physically and emotionally, as his mother. Thiel decides that for the boy's sake he must remarry—this at least is what he tells his pastor. He marries Lene, a physically imposing and abusive woman who is the exact opposite of his first wife. Lene also bears him a son. As Thiel becomes aware of Lene's abuse of Tobias, he begins to unravel. The day after he witnesses a verbal and physical beating, the whole family goes to Thiel's rail house—a forested world he clearly has reserved for the memory of Minna. There Thiel goes to check the line and leaves Lene in charge of Tobias. She neglects her duty, and Tobias "war unter den Zug geraten und wurde zwischen den Rädern wie ein Gummiball

22. Maurer, *Gerhart Hauptmann*, 133.

hin und her geworfen" ([fell] under the train and [was] thrown back and forth between the wheels like a rubber ball, *BT* 58).[23] After this gruesome incident, the tempo of Thiel's disintegration picks up greatly. The evening following Tobias's death, Thiel bludgeons his wife, who has apparently changed for the better after the tragic accident with Tobias, and cuts his infant child's throat.

All critics who write about this novella acknowledge the centrality of the railway as the key to understanding the horrific fate that Thiel and his family suffer. But not all agree on the interpretation of the train as a literary device. Mahr identifies the train as the root cause of Thiel's psychological and spiritual demise.[24] He sees the train as an external, social factor, and this is in keeping with a traditional naturalist interpretation. Heinimann and Martini, by contrast, present a more internal, metaphysical interpretation. Heinimann identifies the train as a metaphor for the unstoppable and the destructive.[25] Martini carries Heinimann's point further when he identifies the train "als eine Art Mythos . . . geschaffen durch die Phantasie des Dichters. [Die Bahn] wird Symbol . . . einer Gewalt, die neben die mythische Gewalt der Natur tritt" (as a type of myth . . . created in the fantasy of the poet-author. The train becomes a symbol . . . of a power that appears next to the mythical power of nature).[26] For these two critics, the train is above all a symbolic representation of Thiel's internal state.

Which interpretation lies closer to the truth? Mahr is partly correct—there is of course some degree of socioeconomic criticism in *Bahnwärter Thiel*. For example, the passengers on the train obviously enjoy a better standard of living than Thiel's. But

---

23. All *Bahnwärter Thiel* excerpts are from Hauptmann's *Sämtliche Werke*, comp. Hans-Egon Hass (Berlin: Propyläen, 1963), 6:35–67.
24. Mahr, *Eisenbahnen in der deutschen Dichtung*, 161.
25. Heinimann, *Technische Innovation*, 246.
26. Fritz Martini, *Das Wagnis der Sprache: Interpretationen deutscher Prosa von Nietzsche bis Benn* (Stuttgart: Ernst Klett, 1956), 89.

there is no indication that Thiel feels particularly burdened by his lot. In fact, contrary to how a true naturalist work would depict working conditions, Hauptmann seems to suggest that Thiel rather enjoys his work. Once again Mahr's analysis is too superficial. Martini and Heinimann come closer to the mark when they allude to the mythical, almost fateful nature of the train as a parallel to Thiel's inner state, but Martini does not go far enough. The train as a symbol of the technological world does not simply step in *next* to the mythical violence of nature; it is part and parcel of that myth. As in "Im Nachtzug," Hauptmann does not employ some bold, unique imagery to describe the brave new world of technology. He draws on the very same range of metaphor, imagery, and symbol that he uses to describe the "Mondscheinreich" (empire of moonshine) in his poem.

The same can be said of the literary form he chose. Unlike Arno Holz and Johannes Schlaf, who attempted to implement new techniques of form for their analysis of the psychological destruction of an individual in *Papa Hamlet* (1889), Hauptmann chose the novella—a form that hearkens all the way back to Bocaccio's *Decameron* (1470). He employs all of the characteristics of the traditional German novella. It contains a Goethian "unerhörte Begebenheit" (unheard-of occurrence). His son is violently run over by a train. It contains, as Tieck would have it, an identifiable turning point, his witnessing of Lene's severe abuse of Tobias. And, of course, it contains the Heysian falcon—Tobias's little brown cap. There is nothing groundbreaking here. New technology has not provided the impetus for a new literary form. This is true despite that fact that Hauptmann's work is a "novellistische Studie," as the subtitle proclaims. But it is no more a scientific study of human consciousness than, for example, is Tieck's *Der blonde Eckbert (Eckbert the Fair)* (1797). Phillip Walther's coming to dinner, meeting Bertha, and uttering the name Strohmian is not radically different from Lene's working the field next to the rail house that contains a shrine to Minna—two worlds that were meant to be kept apart collide, and the result is destruction.

Destruction, specifically that of Thiel's family, is alluded to from the start. Hauptmann reaches far back into the world of mythology to hint at Thiel's eventual unraveling. He describes the protagonist as Herculean in form. Thousands of years before *Bahnwärter Thiel,* Euripides wrote a tragedy entitled *Herakles* (ca. 450 B.C.E.). In this lesser-known drama, Hera drives Hercules to insanity. He thereupon murders his wife and sons in the same manner that Thiel does. Clouser points out other parallels: "Herakles neglects his dependents, just as Thiel neglects Tobias. Thiel's and Herakles' insanities are described in similar length and detail. The murders of both families take place in their own homes and are reported by a messenger. . . . Both Herakles and Thiel think of God in their distress. The Greek hero blames Hera for his fate. . . . Thiel also looks to God in his spiritual derangement but finds no divine answer."[27] Hercules' role in *Bahnwärter Thiel* is similar to the role of classical mythology in general in "Im Nachtzug." It suggests a level of universal inner determinism that far surpasses the social determinism suggested by socialist critics of the industrial era. Clouser sees this inner determinism as similar to the role the gods played in classical mythology, only more isolating. He describes it as "modern man's burden: to rouse his own lonely strength as a spiritual, ethical being."[28] The psychological forces that combine to determine Thiel's lot are as strong as the fate of the gods and stronger than those forces imposed by milieu and the industrialist bent of the era.

The depiction of the train as a symbol of burgeoning industrialism is rather interesting in *Bahnwärter Thiel.* In the pivotal scene most critics analyze, the railway and all things associated with it are described with nature imagery. The wires of the telegraph are like the web of a gigantic spider. The tracks begin to

---

27. Clouser, "Spiritual Malaise," 106.
28. Ibid.

glow like fiery snakes. Then the train arrives with "Keuchen und Brausen" (panting and roaring, *BT* 49), and the earth shakes. It is the arrival of a mythic force of nature. Tellingly, Hauptmann repeats the scene two pages later with the arrival of the storm. "Ein Brausen und Sausen füllte [Thiels] Ohr . . . die ganze Atmosphäre [war] überflutend, dröhnend, schütternd, und brausend. . . . Die Scheiben klirrten, die Erde erbebte" (A roaring and thundering filled Thiel's ear . . . the whole atmosphere was overflowing, booming, shaking, and roaring. . . . The windows rattled, the earth quaked, *BT* 51–52). This storm scene is so similar to the arrival of the train that it is difficult not to conclude that Hauptmann meant to imply that the train, a human invention, is nevertheless an extension of nature, not very different from the storm. This is in accord with Sternberger's construct, which posits that the train was not only "'epoch-making' . . . it was also, if the expression be permitted, 'nature-making.'"[29] It also mirrors Hauptmann's own depiction of the train in "Im Nachtzug" as coming out of Chaos and thus sharing a common heritage with human beings and all other life.

The same equation of nature and technology repeats itself later, only in this case it involves a natural being. When Lene finally makes her way out to Thiel's field to do some planting, she is described as working with "der Geschwindigkeit und Ausdauer einer Maschine" (the speed and stamina of a machine). What ties her to the train and the storm is that she works with "keuchender . . . Brust" (a panting . . . chest, *BT* 56). Clouser points out even more similarities between Lene and the train. Her continual punishment of Tobias intensifies "like an advancing locomotive." Clouser also points out the association of the spider-web-like telegraph wires and the railway itself with Lene: "Eine Kraft schien von dem Weibe auszugehen, unbezwingbar, unentrinnbar, der Thiel sich nicht gewachsen fühlte. Leicht gleich einem feinen Spinngewebe und doch fest wie ein Netz

---

29. Sternberger, *Panorama of the Nineteenth Century*, 42.

von Eisen legte es sich um ihn, fesselnd, überwindend, erschlaffend" (A power seemed to resonate from the woman, unconquerable, inescapable. It was a power to which Thiel did not feel equal. It surrounded him lightly like a fine spider web and yet so firmly like a net of iron that captivates, overwhelms, makes one limp, *BT* 47).[30] Thus Lene as a manifestation of nature is equated with technology, and it is the sounds and look of nature and machine that tie them together in a most threatening way. All three of these, train, Lene, and storm, are manifestations of nature that reflect Thiel's destruction.

It is simply too reductive to say that the train "causes" Thiel's breakdown, as Mahr suggests. The train is, rather, the reflection of Thiel's extraordinary unraveling. Nowhere is this clearer than in the scene in which Thiel's hallucinatory vision of Minna is punctuated by the arrival of the train. Here the train is described as an "Ungetüm" (monster) with bloody "Glotzaugen" (goggle eyes, *BT* 53). Clouser argues that "by making the train into a predator, Hauptmann symbolically frees the machine from its cage—the rails—and replaces the rational concept 'train, servant of man' with a rampaging beast that will mutilate men." He concludes that the train is a "disguised phantom . . . of [Thiel's] guilty conscience."[31] While it may be a bit of an overstatement to say that Thiel's guilty conscience alone drives him to his terrible act, it is clear that the train represents some aspect of Thiel's consciousness. And at some point after Tobias's death, the killer will no longer be the train but Thiel himself.

Christianity is another manifestation of the old mythological narrative bound up in the new. Thiel is a spiritual man. He attends church regularly, he talks to God, and he declares the land by his station holy land. It therefore comes as no surprise that on the walk he and Tobias take just before Tobias's death, "objects of modern technology take on, contrary to their previous omi-

---

30. Clouser, "Spiritual Malaise," 103.
31. Ibid.

nousness in the tale, a spiritual aura."[32] Hauptmann describes Thiel and Tobias as they stand "um den wunderbaren Lauten zu lauschen, die aus dem Holze [der Telegraphenstangen] wie sonore Choräle aus dem Innern einer Kirche hervorströmten" (listening to the wondrous sounds streaming forth from the wood of the telegraph poles like sonorous chorales pouring forth from the interior of a church, *BT* 56). The poles on the south end have a special accord, which Thiel imagines to be "ein Chor seliger Geister" (a chorus of holy spirits, *BT* 57). As in "Im Nachtzug," any attempt by the new worldview to drown out the old appears to fail. It may seem that it has won, but this victory is superficial. The lifeblood of religion pulses just beneath this man-made structure, much like the biblical transfiguration reference in "Im Nachtzug." Hauptmann hammers home this point several lines later, when he gives us Tobias's view of God. "'Vater, ist das der liebe Gott?' fragte der Kleine plötzlich, auf ein braunes Eichhörnchen deutend" ("Father, is that our loving God?" asked the little one suddenly, pointing to a brown squirrel, *BT* 57). God is in the telegraph poles, a means of communication for the railway system, just as God is in the creatures we traditionally associate with nature. Not surprisingly, God is also in Tobias, a name of Hebrew and Greek origin meaning "God is good."

The parallels are unmistakable. Like the reference to the biblical transfiguration in "Im Nachtzug," the enchantment of all things in heaven and on earth means that mythological narrative in its classical or Christian form is far from dead. In fact, human beings must by their very nature use myth in order to tell their tale. The unsolvable conflicts Mahr sees can be resolved after all. Just as the railway ultimately becomes an extension of the application of power in the late nineteenth and twentieth centuries, it also eventually becomes a part of a larger mythological narrative, fitting in as comfortably as a strong thunderstorm and beginning to create myths of its own.

32. Ibid., 104.

[6]

MAX EYTH

Steckt keine Poesie in der Lokomotive, die brausend durch die Nacht zieht und über die zitternde Erde hintobt, als wollte sie Raum und Zeit zermalmen, in dem hastigen, aber wohl geregelten Zucken und Zerren ihrer gewaltigen Glieder, in dem stieren, nur auf ein Ziel losstürmenden Blick ihrer roten Augen, in dem emsigen, willenlosen Gefolge der Wagen, die kreischend und klappernd, aber mit unfehlbarer Sicherheit dem verkörperten Willen aus Eisen und Stahl folge leisten?

Is there no poetry in the locomotive roaring through the night and charging over the quivering earth as if it wanted to crush time and space? Is there no poetry in the hasty but regular jerking and tugging of its powerful limbs, in the stare of its red eyes that never lose sight of their goal? Is there no poetry in the bustling, will-less retinue of cars that follow, screeching and clattering with unmistakable surety, the steel and iron embodiment of will?

Max Eyth, "Poesie und Technik" (Poetry and Technology) (1904)

Like Fontane, the former pharmacist, Max Eyth came to his writing career rather late in life from an unrelated field. He was sixty years old when he moved from Berlin to Ulm to be with his aging mother and began his career as a writer. This phase of his life started in 1896 and ended with his death in 1906. It is what he did before this final phase of his life that makes him of particular interest to this project. Although both his father and grandfather were men of letters, "Altphilologen, Theologen der tüchtigen schwäbischen Art" (old philologists, theologians of the capable Swabian type), Eyth, for the first sixty years of his life, chose a different route. He was educated as a machine engineer at the Polytechnic Institute of Stuttgart. In 1861 he traveled abroad to England, the center of the engineering world at the time. In 1863 he found employment in the factory of John Fowler, a manufacturer of what was to become a revolutionary farm implement, the steam-driven plow. His employment with Fowler lasted nineteen years, during which he traveled the globe from Egypt to America finding new markets for Fowler's modern, technological approach to farming.[1] In 1882, tired of the constant travel, Eyth returned to Germany, specifically to Berlin, and in 1884 founded the German Agricultural Society, an organization devoted to supporting the German farmer. He continued this work until his retirement in Ulm, where he began to write fiction.

As a writer, Eyth has had no lasting impact on the German literary canon. His importance to this work lies in the fact that he is the only poet-engineer of the group. As such, he approaches fiction from a perspective entirely different from that of the other authors I have discussed. Eyth's major work, *Berufstragik* (1899), was his attempt to demythologize the collapse of the bridge over the Firth of Tay in Scotland in 1879. According to Segeberg, Eyth aimed to combine a history of technology with a work of literary fiction.[2] His work, as some critics have pointed out, stands in great contrast to Fontane's famous ballad, "Die

---

1. Theodor Heuss, *Deutsche Gestalten: Studien zum 19. Jahrhundert* (Stuttgart: Wunderlich, 1951), 306–10.

2. Harro Segeberg, *Literarische Technik-Bilder: Studien zum Verhältnis von Technik- und Literaturgeschichte im 19. und frühen 20. Jahrhundert* (Tübingen: Niemeyer, 1987), 139.

Brück' am Tay" (The Bridge over the Tay) (1880), which deals with the same incident. A key difference between the two works is that Eyth felt it was his task to show the beauty inherent in science and technology, as Auerbach had done before him in "Ein Tag in der Heimat." Eyth, like Auerbach, emphasized that technology did not sound the death knell of poetry but in fact generated its own poetry. A look at Eyth's essay "Poesie und Technik" (1904) makes it clear that he wished to establish science and technology as realms that have the ability to produce their own poetry, independent of what he would have considered obsolete mythological narratives.

"Poesie und Technik"

In 1905 Eyth published a series of lectures entitled *Lebendige Kräfte (Living Forces)*. The general intent of these lectures was to demonstrate the nature of the living powers driving his era. He wanted to show that technology served not only material progress but also the intellectual and spiritual development of humankind. He was a forerunner, albeit unwittingly, of C. P. Snow, in that he saw technology as the root cause of a give-and-take between the spiritual/intellectual realm and the material world.[3] Thus, like many before him, he emphasized the dichotomy between the scientific and the mythological. Eyth did not, however, intend his work to affect the world of German letters with revolutionary force. In a commentary on his essays, Kurt Möser argues that Eyth saw his essays as a means to an end—as a contribution to a kind of literature that was functional and pragmatic and in keeping with the aims of the technology movement.[4] He was not the polemicist that Bölsche was but, like

---

3. Max Eyth, "Foreword," *Lebendige Kräfte: Sieben Vorträge aus dem Gebiete der Technik* (Berlin: Springer, 1905), v.

4. Kurt Möser, "Max Eyths Technikthematisierung im Kontext der Technikdebatte," *Anstösse* 32 (1985): 105.

Bölsche, he did assert the primacy of technology through his fiction.

Eyth developed this idea most clearly in "Poesie und Technik," originally written as a speech to the *Verein Deutscher Ingenieure* (Association of German Engineers) in Frankfurt in 1904. The essay begins by debunking the theory that the spirit of poetry would be destroyed by technological and industrial advances. "[I]n der gebildeten Welt, vornehmlich aber in der deutschen gebildeten Welt, der Gedanke feststeht, daß Technik und Poesie zwei sich widersprechende Begriffe sind, zwischen denen eine Berührung nicht denkbar ist" (In the educated world, above all in the German educated world, the idea still holds true that technology and poetry are two contradictory terms between which a connection is unthinkable, PT 3). Here Eyth anticipates Snow's concept of a "third culture" and addresses the fear Auerbach voiced almost thirty years earlier in "Ein Tag in der Heimat," which still seems to exist. That is, technology and poetry are locked in a battle for supremacy from which only one will emerge victorious. Eyth thought that most authors approached the modern technological world with an unnecessarily jaded eye. He called Rosegger "einen der besten unserer Zeit" (one of the best of our age, PT 21); but even Rosegger saw only the costs of technological progress—"Luxus, Geldgier, Verschwendung, Entartung und Sünde" (luxury, greed, waste, degeneration, and sin). "Daß all das Große um uns her nicht entstanden sein kann ohne geniales Schaffen, ohne eisernen Fleiß, ohne heldenmütige Arbeit und Entsagung, ist ein Gedanke, der sein Verdammungsurteil nicht stört," says Eyth (That all of the greatness surrounding us cannot have been created without ingenious works, without iron diligence, without heroic work and renunciation, is a thought that never disturbs his damning judgment, PT 21). In Eyth's view, his contemporaries either mistook technology as the road to ruin or saw it as an unsuitable subject for literature.

Eyth set out to correct these errors by reminding his readers what the word *Technik* (technology) really means. Technology is anything to which the human will gives corporeal form—indeed, he argued, despite technology's material origins it retains an air of infinite boundlessness generally associated with the spiritual world (PT 3–4). Here Eyth seems to lend an air of the religious and mythological to technology.

And how could technology be incompatible with poetry, when poetry is only "was uns den geistigen Gehalt der uns umgebenden Körperwelt offenbart" (the revealed nonmaterial content of the surrounding corporeal world, PT 4)? The difficulty here is the problematic nature of the word *geistig,* which, among other things, can mean both *intellectual* and *spiritual.* I have translated it as "nonmaterial" in order to get around this difficulty. In this way, Eyth suggests that all physical objects contain within themselves something nonphysical, something nonmaterial. This idea is hardly new with Eyth, of course, nor does he go so far as to suggest that mythology is the basis of technology. But Eyth is suggesting that Eucken's worries about the soul of humanity are misplaced. Perhaps there is no great divide between the world of technology and the world of the *Geist.*

Eyth follows the ancients in defining the three characteristics of poetry as truth, goodness, and beauty (PT 7–8). But he associates these attributes also with technology, which is good in its service to mankind, beautiful in perfectly and unconsciously reducing man's burden, and (most important for my purposes) true, because it directly relates to Eyth's concept of realism. As far is Eyth is concerned, poetry without truth is oxymoronic; all poetry that deserves the name is by definition true, and for Eyth this means that it is a faithful representation of reality. For something to be true, be it technology or art, it must accord with the eternal laws of nature and reality (PT 6). The reference to "eternal laws" echoes Rosegger most obviously, but also Bölsche to a great extent. In fact, Eyth's reference to the eternal laws of nature echoes Bölsche's title, *Die naturwissenschaftlichen Grundlagen der Poesie.* While Eyth does not suggest that poets should become scientists, he does imply that literature, like science, should follow the laws of nature and, in the words of Bölsche, let go of their earlier, mistaken beliefs.[5]

But Eyth avoids Bölsche's dogmatic, one-sided view of science by acknowledging the mythological roots of technological innovation. Technological advances have impressed the world with their scientific foundations, yes, but at the same time their power is akin to the power of Germanic legends, or even Indian and Arabian fairytales. This is as clear a statement on the relationship between technology and mythology as one will find in Eyth. In the same passage he refers to photography, rail and steamboat travel, and telegraphy, none of which existed a mere seventy years before he wrote. The ideas that underlie these technologies were, according to him, merely the myths from which all technology ultimately springs.

The constellation of nature, myth, and technology leads us back to Sternberger, who argued that technological manifestations like the train did not destroy nature but became part of it. Neither vanquished nor victor, they are more like allies, each maintaining its own prestige.[6] Eyth, who concludes his essay with a call not to serve nature but to rule it, would not go as far as Sternberger, but he clearly saw the links between technology and nature. In fact, he maintained, technology belongs to the earth in the truest sense. It is a part of nature, and inasmuch as both technology and mythology are about naming, identifying, and controlling, and thus about power, nature ties them together. Nature is both the source of technology and mythology and that which both would conquer. "Auf Wissen und Können, auf Wort und Werkzeug beruht die Macht, die den nackten, wehrlosen Menschen zum Herrscher über alles Lebende auf Erden gemacht hat, die den Zwerg zum Sieger im Riesenkampf mit den Gewalten der Natur bestimmte" (Power rests on

---

5. Bölsche, *Grundlagen der Poesie*, 5.
6. Sternberger, *Panorama of the Nineteenth Century*, 42–43.

knowledge and ability, on words and tools that have made naked, defenseless mankind into the ruler over all living things on earth, and that declared the dwarf [man] victor in the terrific struggle with the forces of nature, PT 15). Words and tools, that is, myth and technology, are what determine power. And both are equally powerful in their struggle with nature.

"Die Brück' am Tay"

In *Berufstragik,* Eyth painstakingly depicts the struggle between nature and engineer in great detail. While the work does not deal with the train per se, its subject is the construction of a bridge that is to serve as a rail line. Mahr suggests that Eyth succeeds in pinning the blame for the collapse of the bridge on working conditions, the engineer's personal problems, and technical problems with the construction of the piers.[7] If this were the case, Eyth would have written a nicely crafted, demythologized work of historical fiction that would have stood in stark contrast to Fontane's ballad on the bridge. But his story is about more than the things Mahr lists, and in fact the work does not vary greatly from that of Fontane.

The subject of these two works, the bridge over the Firth of Tay, which was to be the pride of all British engineering, was completed in February 1878. It was approximately three kilometers long, which made it the longest bridge in the world at the time. The trouble with the span was that cost efficiency seemed to be the overriding construction principle. According to Segeberg, the bridge was light in its construction, made of inexpensive materials, of inadequate height and width, connected with the wrong kind of bolts, and lacking reinforcing piers at either end.[8]

7. Mahr, *Eisenbahnen in der deutschen Dichtung,* 168.
8. Segeberg, *Literarische Technik-Bilder,* 132.

In June 1878 the span was finally considered safe enough for passenger rail travel, but with the stipulation that passenger trains not exceed twenty-five miles per hour. Confidence in this inexpensively and lightly constructed span began to wane in the winter of 1879. This was a particularly cold winter, and the iron in the bridge began to crack; the connector bolts were snapping in the freezing temperatures. The problems were not corrected, however, and disaster struck on December 28, 1879, when the Edinburgh Express crossed the bridge carrying seventy-five passengers and exceeding the recommended speed limit by fifteen miles per hour. The evening was stormy, with gale-force winds of more than seventy miles per hour. At 7:14 P.M., just as the Express was attempting to cross, the winds succeeded in destroying the bridge. The train drove off the broken section of bridge, and all seventy-five passengers perished in the frigid waters of the Tay.

Both Fontane and Eyth created notable works of literature about the tragedy. In order to gain a deeper understanding of Eyth's work, it will be helpful to begin with Fontane's ballad, penned in January 1880, a mere two weeks after the collapse (see Appendix B). This ballad, not an unusual form for Fontane at that point in his career, is an interesting amalgamation of images from the event itself and from Fontane's creative imagination. Significantly, it begins and ends with the witches from Shakespeare's *Macbeth*. Segeberg does not like Fontane's use of the witches; he would prefer that the historical, technical aspects not be subsumed in fateful, tragic exaggeration. He finds it distressing that modern interpreters would compare a manmade disaster with mystical forces of nature.[9] Chambers also thinks the witches are a mistake; had Fontane simply dropped the epigram that begins the poem and made the voices "less tangible and recognizable," the work would have been much more effective. Chambers does ultimately find it "interesting that Fontane made

9. Ibid., 129.

this not entirely disastrous attempt to reconcile the two worlds of the supernatural past and scientific present."[10] Nature and technology are most certainly at odds with each other; Fontane's ballad does not bear out Sternberger's view that the two realms can be brought together and coexist on friendly terms.[11] In Fontane's poem, their relationship is one of enmity. It is certain from the outset that there will be a victor and a vanquished, and that the witches, symbolizing mythologized nature, will prevail and destroy the train.

The ballad's formal structure itself shows the dissonance between nature and technology. The middle five stanzas follow the standard ballad form—they are all eight-line stanzas with a regular rhythm and a rhyme scheme that includes four rhymed pairs. The opening and closing of the witches' dialogue (lines 1–16 and 58–69), by contrast, are irregularly formed.[12] Heinimann notes that the tension between nature and technology—the tension, that is, between chaos and apparent order—is expressed in the contrast between the irregular stanzas of the witches and the strictly structured stanzas of the ballad's main body.[13] The chaos serves to destroy the orderliness of the ballad, and there is no implicit hope for a conciliatory note, as there is, for example, in Hauptmann's "Im Nachtzug."

The antagonism between nature and technology evident in the poem's form is also apparent in the content. On the one hand are the witches, who in their *Schadenfreude* plan and then celebrate their destruction of the bridge and the train. On the other hand, in keeping with the tradition of the ballad, Fontane has given us a "hero" in the engineer, Johnie, who utters the triumphant lines celebrating technology. Johnie is confident that

---

10. Chambers, *Supernatural and Irrational Elements*, 48.

11. Sternberger, *Panorama of the Nineteenth Century*, 42.

12. All "Brück' am Tay" excerpts are from *Romane, Erzählungen, Gedichte,* sec. 1, vol. 6 of Fontane's *Sämtliche Werke,* ed. Walter Keitel (Munich: Hanser, 1964), 285–87. See Appendix B for the poem in German.

13. Heinimann, *Technische Innovation,* 277.

the fierce gale raging outside will be no match for the superior technology of the bridge, and that he will bring his train safely home and celebrate a belated Christmas with his family (the belated Christmas celebration was surely added to intensify the sentimentality, a common characteristic of the ballad). "Ein fester Kessel, ein doppelter Dampf, / Die bleiben Sieger in solchem Kampf" (A firm boiler, double steam, / They remain victors in such a battle, lines 37–38). "Sieger" (victor) and "Kampf" (battle) suggest confrontation and conflict; thus the antagonistic relationship is reinforced not only by the witches but by man as well, for Johnie is out to do battle just like the witches. In the fourth balladic stanza he praises the bridge and expresses his disdain for earlier times, when the bay was not fordable even by boat. In the end, however, Johnie loses the struggle and dies in three laconic lines: "Und jetzt, als ob Feuer vom Himmel fiel' / Erglüht es in niederschießender Pracht / Überm Wasser unten . . . Und wieder ist Nacht" ("And now, as if fire fell from the heavens / It glowed in shooting splendor / Over the water below . . . and again it is night, lines 55–57).[14] His death is distinctly unheroic.

If Johnie and the train are the "heroes" of the piece, as Heinimann suggests, then, inasmuch as they are both destroyed, the ballad loses any touch of the heroic. It becomes instead an expression of the impotence of the individual at the very moment in history when humankind has significantly increased its power through technology. Technological progress had the effect of making individual heroism irrelevant.[15] Fontane seems to be suggesting that estrangement from nature through technology has sapped our potential for a more poetic form of heroism.

Martini characterizes "Die Brück' am Tay," with its critical

---

14. Fritz Martini, "Theodor Fontane, 'Die Brück' am Tay,'" in *Wege zum Gedicht: Interpretationen von Balladen,* ed. Rupert Hirschenauer and Albrecht Weber (Munich: Schnell and Steiner, 1963), 389.

15. Heinimann, *Technische Innovation,* 278.

view of technology, as transitional in more than one sense. The ballad stands "zwischen Altem und Neuem, Geschichtlichem und Gegenwärtigem" (between old and new, historical and present). It expresses both Fontane's own transitional status, as an author bridging the realists and the moderns, and the rapidly changing literary landscape of the latter half of the nineteenth century.[16] This conclusion is problematic for my contention that many of these transitional works depict the present by using the past as part and parcel of present. Fontane's ballad does not fit neatly into my schema; the dialectic of enlightenment and myth that I am arguing for does not seem to inform "Die Brück' am Tay." No mythology seems to underlie the train or the bridge as manifestations of technology. The realms of witches and train remain distinctly separate.

At the same time, the poem does seem clearly to reject Eucken's thesis that technology will be the death of poetry. Inasmuch as the witches in "Die Brück' am Tay" are mythological figures, they represent poetry in Eucken's sense of the word, and they are potent enough to destroy the technological wonder that was the bridge over the Firth of Tay. In Fontane's account, myth wins out. But Fontane does have something in common with both Camphausen and Eucken. His ballad suggests that the world of mythology and the world of technology are two distinct and irreconcilable realms. But "Die Brück' am Tay" is an early work, and Fontane had not yet grown into the skilled author he ultimately became with later novels like *Cécile* and *Effi Briest*.

Berufstragik

Despite its publication date of 1880, critics often see "Die Brück' am Tay" as a work that lacks an appropriately modern

---

16. Martini, "Theodor Fontane, 'Die Brück' am Tay,'" 390–92.

depiction of science and technology. Mahr sees the ballad as a clear statement that human invention is no match for the force of nature.[17] Segeberg bemoans what he considers Fontane's simplistic approach to this question.[18] Heinimann lauds the ballad as a comment on human hubris and the disillusionment that inevitably follows.[19] Virtually all of the critics agree that nature and technology were seen as competing powers in Fontane's day. Heinimann argues that contemporaries saw no common root of nature and technology. As I have tried to show, however, the evidence suggests a different possibility.

Mahr and Heinimann see Eyth's *Berufstragik* as something entirely different from Fontane's ballad. Mahr, as we have seen, thinks that Eyth explains the collapse of the bridge in terms of working conditions, squabbles between the engineers, and technical problems with the bridge's supports—things outside Fontane's understanding.[20] Heinimann too sees only the contrasts between Fontane's poem and Eyth's novella; Eyth's work, he says, was written from a "rational-causal" point of view.[21] I disagree that *Berufstragik* is a work of disenchantment or disillusionment. Eyth, although he may not have said so in his essays, demonstrates a third-culturalist's sensitivity in his fiction.

Segeberg is the only critic to point out some of the very obvious similarities between the two works, though he does so hesitantly. "Bis in Einzelheiten hinein stellte der Erzähler dadurch klar, wer am Ende wirklich handelt. Als Stoß [der Hauptingenieur] den Unglückszug bestieg, heißt es: 'Stoß sprang ein, und der Sturm schlug sie [die Waggontür] zu'" (Down to the last detail, the narrator makes it clear which forces are at work in the end. As Stoß [the chief engineer] boards the unlucky train, it is described thus: "Stoß jumped in, and the

---

17. Mahr, *Eisenbahnen in der deutschen Dichtung*, 168.
18. Segeberg, *Literarische Technik-Bilder*, 127–28.
19. Heinimann, *Technische Innovation*, 279.
20. Mahr, *Eisenbahnen in der deutschen Dichtung*, 168–69.
21. Heinimann, *Technische Innovation*, 279.

storm slammed [the passenger car door] shut").[22] Segeberg sees this personification of nature, and this personalizing of the struggle, as the key to understanding Eyth's work. "Das animistisch-naturhafte Konfliktmuster hat am Ende eindeutig obsiegt. Der Brückenerbauer, der die lebendige Natur verletzt hat, muß mit dem eigenen Leben büßen; das Bauopfer, seitens der Arbeiter bereits erbracht, genügt nicht" (The animistic-natural pattern of conflict is clearly victorious. The bridge builder, who wronged living nature, has to atone with his own life; the sacrifice of the building on the part of the workers . . . is not enough).[23] Thus Eyth's project does not appear to differ greatly from that of Fontane. In fact, the key difference lies not in the disenchantment of the event but in the recognition of the shared root of technology and myth—and in this way Eyth's approach is more sophisticated than Fontane's.

Eyth tells essentially the same story that Fontane does, but he makes himself the first-person narrator of a work of historical fiction. Eyth begins with an account of his travels to England in search of employment as an engineer. He stays in a boarding house with another German engineer and an Austrian engineer who are also looking for work. They all find positions, but there is a distinct hierarchical aspect to their success. Schindler, the German, fails to find an engineering job and becomes a French teacher in an English boarding school and later in a German high school. Eyth himself finds work in the budding field of industrial agriculture, which will serve as the impetus for his world travels. The third engineer, the Austrian Harold Stoß, finds employment with William Bruce, owner of a civil engineering firm and member of the directorate of the "Nordflintshire Eisenbahn" (North Flintshire Railway, B 427).[24] Stoß thus sets

22. Segeberg, *Literarische Technik-Bilder,* 169.
23. Ibid.
24. It is important to note that Eyth felt it necessary to change the names of the principal figures involved in the tragedy. This includes not only the human characters but also the Edinburger Railway, which becomes the

out on the path of building the longest span bridge in the world.

We learn of Stoß's successes, setbacks, and ultimate destruction partly in the form of letters between Stoß and Eyth and the letters given to Eyth by Stoß's wife, Billy Bruce, daughter of his employer, William Bruce. Eyth tells us through these letters, and in an account of two meetings with Stoß after the construction of the bridge, that Stoß was always worried about his mathematical calculations concerning the force of the wind in the bay area. Despite these concerns, and despite two major accidents that occur during construction, the bridge is completed. For Stoß, however, it is never truly finished. Because of his worries about his questionable calculations, he begins to deteriorate both physically and mentally. Stoß's condition becomes so serious that his wife, Billy Bruce, implores Eyth to talk him into taking a long vacation with his family. Eyth succeeds in this, but they part ways with Stoß boarding the ill-fated train.

Eyth makes the interesting narrative choice of making himself a fictional character in the novella. Segeberg has established that Eyth was in no way connected with any such figures as Schindler and Stoß during his early years in England, and he certainly did not know personally any of the engineers affiliated with the Tay bridge.[25] But Eyth adopts the realist posture of denying the artificiality of his fiction. As Furst puts it, the realist novel "stakes its claim to special authenticity by accepting its primary allegiance to experience over art, thus purporting to capture truth."[26] To give the work an air of authenticity, Eyth includes actual autobiographical events such as his trip to England, his work with the steam-driven plow, his world travels, and so on.[27] Narrator and author are presented as identical. To strength-

---

"Nordflintshire Eisenbahn," and the Firth of Tay, which becomes the "Ennobucht."

25. Segeberg, *Literarische Technik-Bilder,* 140.
26. Furst, *All Is True,* 6.
27. Segeberg, *Literarische Technik-Bilder,* 141.

en this air of authenticity and credibility, Eyth announces in a footnote "daß sämtliche Namen, auch die Ortsnamen, die sich in irgendwelcher Weise auf die 'Ennobrücke' beziehen, aus naheliegenden Gründen erfunden sind. Dagegen ist die technische Geschichte des Unternehmens auch im einzelnen den Tatsachen entsprechend erzählt" (that all of the names, including place names related to the Enno Bridge, have, for obvious reasons, been changed. By contrast, the technical history of the undertaking is related in exact detail, B 427). The name changes are therefore the only adulterations of "truth" he is wiling to concede.

The narrative repeatedly reminds the reader of its faithfulness to the truth. When, for example, the narrator coincidentally runs into Stoß and his wife in Vienna, he interrupts the story to admonish the reader not to hope that Schindler too will appear. This would happen only "im erbärmlichsten Roman" (in the most wretched of novels), because only bad novels follow such predictable paths; Eyth's work, by contrast, faithfully represents life's difficulties in all their messy and unpredictable particularity (B 467). Eyth repeatedly alludes to the truthfulness of his account. During the night of the storm, for example, the narrator reaches for a glass that he is convinced he already filled and finds it empty. The implication is that some sort of poltergeist has done some mischief. The narrator hesitates even to relate this incredible incident "in diesem wahrheitsgetreuen Berichte" (in this truthful report, B 534). His use of the word "report" implies an objective, empirical telling of reality.

Eyth, like all realist authors, struggles mightily to simply report "the facts." More than any other author in this study, however, he does attempt to provide a technological explanation for all that occurs, but he does not leave it at that. He provides, for example, remarkably meticulous technical descriptions of the bridge. Stoß relates in objective detail the exact number and composition of the supports, the length and height of the bridge, and the description of the train tracks (B 520). Hard on the heels of this description, however, Eyth resorts to artistic convention. The narrator describes the shadow cast by the bridge as having "einen fast unheimlichen Eindruck" (an almost uncanny impression, B 521), thereby moving the bridge from the world of engineering to the world of the supernatural. Stoß himself refers to the bridge as "das schwarze Ungetüm" (the black monster, B 522), the exact description that lent an air of the supernatural to the train in works such as *Cécile* and *Bahnwärter Thiel*. Thus the bridge moves from the technological into the mythological realm, casting doubt on Heinimann's assessment that Eyth provides us with an entirely "rational-causal interpretation" of the disaster at the Firth of Tay.[28]

Stoß's obsessive concern about his mathematical calculations follows the same pattern of moving from the technological to the mythological. During the construction phase, Stoß understands how little engineers really know when it comes to their calculations, but adds, "Aber wo wäre die Welt geblieben, wenn nicht einige die Nerven gehabt hätten, die es möglich machen, im Dunklen zu greifen?" (But where would the world be if a few had not had the nerve that made it possible to grasp into the dark? B 479). He tries to silence his doubts by telling himself that "die [Bau]formeln fast so lang wie die Pfeiler [wurden] und beweisen sonnenklar, daß der Plan einen glänzenden Erfolg versprach" (the [construction] formulas were almost as long as the piers, and so decidedly clear that the plan promised to be a shining success, B 464). So long, that is, as "die Grundsätze, nach denen ich ... rechnen mußte" (the mathematical assumptions upon which I had to rely, B 464) were correct.

After the bridge is completed, the small cracks in his confidence become yawning crevasses. In Vienna Stoß shares with the narrator his fear that the entire bridge may be built on an erroneous assumption (B 453). "In diesen großen Aufgaben ist noch so vieles dunkel" (In these great tasks, there is much that remains

28. Heinimann, 279.

in the dark, *B* 524), he says, referring explicitly to the bridge calculations but implicitly and more broadly to the technological project itself. Expertise in engineering, he says, has little to do with experience or even instinct; a third, inexplicable and even unfathomable, factor underlies the science of engineering (*B* 457–58). Eyth makes the same point in "Poesie und Technik" when he claims that despite its connectedness to the material world, technology takes something from the boundlessness of the spiritual (PT 4). This is precisely the "unfathomable" and "inexplicable" thing Stoß refers to. Human beings tend to fill the inexplicable gaps in experience with myth, and Eyth, despite his occasional protests to the contrary, is no exception.

The narrator has the final word on the underpinnings of science, and here again myth comes to his aid. He says of the disaster, "Das entsetzliche Unglück weise aufs neue darauf hin, daß es Grenzen gebe, die der Mensch nicht ungestraft überschreite" (The horrific mishap pointed again to the fact that there are limits which humans cannot cross unpunished, *B* 552). The collapse of the bridge cannot be explained merely in terms of mathematical errors.[29] To understand this catastrophe one must go all the way back to original sin. This central concept is alluded to when Stoß meets for the first time the woman who will become his wife, "unter den Riesenblättern eines Bananenbusches" (under the gigantic leaves of a banana tree, *B* 431). "Eine kleine Eva" (a little Eve) received him "in dem Paradiesgarten" (in the Garden of Eden). He is tempted into the world of engineering by his own ambitions and by Billy Bruce, who in this instance plays the part of Eve, who lures Stoß with the promise of expanding his engineering knowledge. Throughout the story he oversteps the bounds of humankind, allowing, as Segeberg suggests, technology to remain overshadowed by original sin.[30]

As we have seen, Stoß begins to pay the price for his hubris

29. Mahr, *Eisenbahnen in der deutschen Dichtung*, 168–69.
30. Segeberg, *Literarische Technik-Bilder*, 171.

long before the actual collapse of the bridge. He feels an intolerable burden on his conscience that he cannot seem to relieve. When the narrator meets Stoß for the first time in years, after the bridge is built, he sees a different person: "Seine Haltung war ersichtlich gebückt; manchmal ... schnellte er mit einem nervösen Ruck in die Höhe. Er war dünner geworden. . . . [Seine] Augen schienen größer als früher, wenn er sie aufschlug ... dann lag etwas wie eine ängstliche Frage in dem Blick. . . . Aber er sah selten auf. . . . Meistens blickte er zu boden. . . . Dann sah man wohl auch seine bleiche Unterlippe sich regen, während die Finger seiner linken Hand in fortwährender Bewegung waren" (His posture was visibly bent; sometimes ... he started with a nervous jerk upward. He had become thinner. . . . [His eyes] appeared bigger than before, and when he opened them there was a fearful question in his glance. . . . But he seldom looked up. . . . Most of the time he glanced at the ground. . . . Then one would see his pale upper lip quivering, while the fingers of his left hand were in constant motion, B 516). Stoß is unraveling in much the same manner as Franz Thiel. Just as the telegraph wires in *Bahnwärter Thiel* are depicted as a spider web, and just as Lene's sexual and emotional power over Thiel lies as lightly as a spider web but as firmly as an iron net, the bridge lies upon Stoß's mind "leicht wie ein Spinngewebe über einem höllischen Abgrund" (light as a spider web over a hellish abyss, B 458). Both men suffer great guilt, Thiel for his perceived betrayal of Minna and his outright betrayal of Tobias, and Stoß for his shoddy construction. And both men are destroyed, directly or indirectly, by a demonized or mythologized version of technology.

Not only does Eyth invest the bridge with mythological importance; he also mythologizes the forces of nature in a way very much in keeping with Fontane's depiction of the tragedy in his ballad. At the start of construction, Stoß describes the bay as "ein geheimnisvoller Hermaphrodit" (a mysterious hermaphrodite, B 471); it is difficult to determine whether it is a river or a bay. And, like Johnie in Fontane's poem, Stoß personalizes his battle to overcome the bay:

> Vorläufig liegt die weite Bucht noch vor uns, im Gold der Abendsonne, als ahnte sie nichts Böses. . . . Es ist, als fühlten die gewaltigen Wassermassen, daß sie hier Herr sind und nichts und niemand . . . ihnen zu widerstehen wagt. Aber es kommt anders, mein guter Enno. In wenigen Jahren stehen achtzig schlanke Pfeiler in deinem Grund gegen die du toben kannst, soviel du Lust hast, und über deiner Tiefe liegt ein eisernes Band, auf dem die Zwerge hin und her fahren. . . . Die Tage deiner Alleinherrschaft sind gezählt.

> For the time being, the bay lay before us in the golden glow of the evening sun, as if it had no notion of anything evil. . . . It is as if the powerful masses of water felt that they were master here and nothing and no one . . . dare stand up to them. But a change is coming, my good Enno. In a few years, eighty thin piers will stand in your bottom, against which you can rage as much as you desire; and across your depths will lie an iron band on which the dwarfs will travel back and forth. . . . The days of your hegemony are numbered. (*B* 472)

Stoß does not quite demonize the bay at this point, but he clearly personifies it, and this whole passage is reminiscent of Johnie in "Die Brück' am Tay," who declares, "Wir kriegen es unter: das Element" (We will beat it back: the element, line 40). Stoß also personalizes the struggle; he makes it a battle between himself and nature. He will win, he thinks, because, as Eyth says in "Poesie und Technik," he believes that technology "[bestimmte] den Zwerg zum Sieger im Riesenkampf mit den Gewalten der Natur" (determined that the dwarf [man] is the victor in the great battle with the forces of nature, PT 15).[31] But the bay reveals its power when the bridge collapses while still under construction, prefiguring its ultimate demise. Studying the site of this initial collapse, Stoß notes that the current in the bay continued to race by, "als habe ihm der ungewohnte Bissen nicht

---

31. Compare the use of Zwerg here to describe humankind and the use of Zwerg in the previous quotation from Berufstragik.

übel geschmeckt" (as if the uncommon bite had not tasted bad, B 501).

Finally, on the night of the storm, the forces of nature, represented by the bay and the gale, are demonized and come into conflict with the train, which itself appears in demonized form. As Stoß and the narrator part ways, a train reminiscent of so many trains from works of this period arrives: "Im gleichen Augenblick schnaubte das schwarze, triesende Ungeheuer mit seinen zwei Feueraugen an uns vorüber" (In the same moment the black, dripping monster with its two eyes of fire snorted past, B 532). The image of the storm slamming the train door after Stoß establishes the conflict between these two demons, nature and technology, but the conflict does not appear to be between something natural and something unnatural. It seems, rather, a conflict between two supernatural, mythologized forces. This is different from "Die Brück' am Tay" but similar to what occurs in *Bahnwärter Thiel,* where the storm and the train are presented in a similar way. The narrator depicts the storm as "ein Wühlen und Wallen, ein Sausen und Seufzen, ein Klatschen und Krachen" (a churning and seething, a roaring and moaning, a clapping and crashing, B 541). The sea tosses in "schwarzer Wut" (black fury), and in order to regain its destructive strength, "Das Unwetter hatte . . . aufs neue Atem geholt" (The storm had . . . newly regained its breath, B 533). Segeberg has it right with regard to this demonization when he posits that it is Eyth's attempt to bear the fear-inducing strangeness of an ever more abstract connection to nature. Myth and science are about controlling our fear of the unknown and inexplicable, and the experience of Stoß and the narrator mimics this process. The difficulty here is that nature, just like the nature depicted in Fontane's "Die Brück' am Tay," "als Manifestation dämonisch-ungebändigter höherer Gewalten stets obsiegt" (is always victorious as a manifestation of unbound demonic higher powers).[32]

32. Segeberg, *Literarische Technik-Bilder,* 155.

In the end, however, the narrator offers an empirical explanation for the disaster. With regard to cost efficiency, he explains, "[Die Geldfrage] reckte sich neben den plötzlich entdeckten technischen Schwierigkeiten wie ein alles erdrückendes Gespenst" ([The question of money] moved up next to the suddenly discovered technical difficulties like an all-encompassing ghost, B 488). On the subject of construction, he notes, "[Die Stangen] sind mit Keilen in den Säulen befestigt, und vom Zittern der Brücke wurden die Keile immer loser ... die ganze Brücke zitterte und schwankte, wenn ein Zug zu rasch darüberging" ([The rods] were fastened to the columns with gussets, and, owing to the shaking of the bridge, the gussets continued to loosen ... the whole bridge shook and swung whenever a new train crossed it too fast, B 539). Another possible explanation is that the extreme wind caused the train to derail (B 551). But none of these explanations takes precedence over the vengeful "ungebändigten, höheren Gewalten" (boundless higher powers) that demand recompense for human hubris (B 552)—for, in effect, re-committing original sin.

In "Poesie und Technik" Eyth writes that modern literature has largely ignored technology, and that when writers do address the subject they tend to depict technology as an agent of misery and social decline. This sweeping claim ignores more than thirty years of literature that takes the intersection of man, technology, and nature as its theme. *Berufstragik* is Eyth's attempt to set the matter right, but he never really differentiates himself from other authors who address the question of technology from a third-culture perspective. The purely technical descriptions of the bridge and the train, as well as the technical explanation of the collapse, do not stand on their own. Eyth mythologizes technology and thus falls under the same paradigm that the other authors in this study do. He cannot help it, for, as Eyth well understood, there are gaps in human understanding, and when humans discover those gaps, they fill them in with myth.

[7]

CONCLUSION

But without myth every culture loses the healthy natural power of its creativity: only a horizon defined by myths completes and unifies a whole cultural movement.

Friedrich Nietzsche, *The Birth of Tragedy* (1872)

This project originated in response to a call by Peter Watson to begin to think of the arts and sciences as part of one extended narrative.[1] This type of prodding has quite a history indeed. Elinor S. Shaffer puts it best in her introduction to a collection of essays she edited, entitled *The Third Culture: Literature and Science* (1998). She notes that with the ascendancy of science and the scientific outlook in the latter half of the nineteenth century, "the need to find a framework in which old values could still guide the new procedures seemed urgent to many."[2] The defenders of the "old values" and the "new procedures" could not have imagined that this need would remain urgent more than a hundred years later, or that the positions they outlined then sparked the beginning of a debate that continues today.

In the twentieth century the debate, as pointed out in the

---

1. Watson, *Modern Mind*, 771.
2. Elinor S. Shaffer, ed. *The Third Culture: Literature and Science* (Berlin: De Gruyter, 1998), 5.

Introduction, was defined in its current terms by C. P. Snow, the British novelist and scientist. His essay "The Two Cultures" (1959) identified an increasingly sharp dichotomy in Western culture. On one side of this divide Snow saw "literary intellectuals," and on the other, "physical scientists."[3] Snow's argument was not new; it was a continuation of a debate that began decades earlier with men like Eucken and Bölsche. Snow's most original thought came in a follow-up essay written four years later, entitled "The Two Cultures: A Second Look," in which he remarked, "it is probably too early to speak of a third culture already in existence. But I am now convinced that this is coming."[4] Snow's lasting contribution to the debate was his call for this "third culture," which he hoped would bridge the gap that he, and many others since, recognized as dangerous "in a time when science is determining much of our destiny, that is, whether we live or die."[5]

The concept really began to take hold in the late 1980s, and since then scores of books have dealt either implicitly or explicitly with this debate. Mahr's 1982 work is an example and Watson's more recent book is another. There is, however, still much confusion about the idea of a third culture. Snow and his successors defined the concept loosely, and few works take the head-on approach of Bowen and Wilson's *Science and Literature: Bridging the Two Cultures* (2001), in which the concept is elucidated through an exchange between a professor of science and professor of literature.[6] Like Bowen and Wilson, Snow wanted to give equal weight to both points of view, but most works on the third culture are not as convincingly argued. Shaffer's volume,

3. Snow, "Two Cultures," 3–4.
4. Snow, "The Two Cultures: A Second Look," in C. P. Snow, *The Two Cultures* (1963; Cambridge: Cambridge University Press, 1993), 70–71.
5. Ibid., 98.
6. Zack Bowen and David L. Wilson, *Science and Literature: Bridging the Two Cultures* (Gainesville: University Press of Florida, 2001).

for example, addresses only thinkers from the humanities. A collection of essays under the title *The Third Culture* (1995) presents only the views of scientists. John Brockmann, the editor of the volume, states, "the third culture consists of those scientists and other thinkers in the empirical world who, through their work and expository writing, are taking the place of the traditional intellectual in rendering visible the deeper meanings of our lives, redefining who and what we are."[7] This collection therefore precludes the humanities.

Edward O. Wilson takes yet another approach to defining the third culture in his *Consilience: The Unity of Knowledge* (1998). Wilson also leans toward the science end of the debate and suggests that someday we shall have no need of a third culture. Someday science will be able to explain everything empirically, from ethics to beauty and even the existence of God.[8] Wilson would have the two cultures become one, which is also what Snow had in mind. But Wilson's third culture, unlike Snow's, would be dominated by the scientific community—not something Snow considered, given that the scientific point of view had not yet attained the hegemony it enjoys today.

Mahr's work on the railway can also be considered a contribution to the third-culture debate, and again one that leans toward the scientific end of the spectrum. Mahr argues in his concluding remarks that humankind must foster "eine strikte Entmythologisierung des poetischen Denkens—des Denkens über die Dichtung ebenso wie des Denkens über die Technik" (a strict demythologizing of poetic thinking—thinking about poetry as well as thinking about technology). This would set literature free to question the essence of humanity in the face

---

7. John Brockmann, ed., *The Third Culture* (New York: Simon and Schuster, 1995), 17.

8. Edward O. Wilson, *Consilience: The Unity of Knowledge* (New York: Knopf, 1998).

of the ever-expanding possibilities created by technological progress.⁹ But, as I have tried to show, Mahr's solution is difficult if not impossible to achieve.

Mahr and the other science-oriented third culturists tend to assume that science and technology either currently do, or will in the future, reflect reality faithfully. My purpose has been to show that science and the technological advances it spawns constitute a form of discourse very similar to the discourse of myth and its literary offspring. As explanatory narratives, both science and poetry are culturally determined systems that represent reality in a specific historical and cultural context. Moreover, both paradigms are, in the words of Wolf Lepenies, "interest determined"; that is, both are subjectively defined systems, devised to help humans understand their world.¹⁰

We need both narratives, because neither one can adequately explain existence by itself. Science cannot tell us everything we need to know about the world, human nature, and the human condition. Even as scientific discovery continues to unfold, there will always be empirical questions that the present state of scientific knowledge cannot answer. Take the example of particle physics today: each time we think we have solved the mystery of atomic structure, someone discovers a new cousin of the quark or neutrino. In the face of the fear engendered by this apparent infinity, humans feel a great need to fill in the gaps. And we tend to do so with myth.

Mahr's suggestion that we demythologize poetry is misguided. We can no more demythologize poetry than we can cease using the internal combustion engine without inventing a replacement that serves the same purpose. Mahr also recommends that we demythologize technology, an equally impossible proposition. As Sternberger points out, "both elements, the natural [poetic] and the artificial [technological], adhere as tightly to

9. Mahr, *Eisenbahnen in der deutschen Dichtung*, 271.
10. Wolf Lepenies, "The Direction of the Disciplines: The Future of the Universities," *Comparative Criticism* 11 (1989): 64.

one another as the Magdeburg hemispheres and are so inextricably enmeshed"[11] that we can only accept the inexorable interdependence of both. This is the essence of the third-culture approach.

As I said in the Introduction, this project was conceived as a contribution to third-culture studies. The works I have analyzed demonstrate the common origin of the poetic and the scientific paradigms and their inevitable interdependence. I have tried to show that Rademacher's categories of thought about technological progress, as represented by various responses to the railway, are not particularly useful in resolving the debate on the relationship between literature and technology. It is not only that Rademacher has no sense of a third culture but that his categories assume the primacy of technology and that he looks forward to the eventual triumph of technology over myth, a triumph that is not borne out in the literature of the era.

It makes more sense to look at literary representations of the train in terms of the layering process described in the Introduction. For example, the concept of the train as harbinger of spiritual chaos that one sees in Rosegger's *Die neue Bahn* is still apparent twenty-five years later in the dark, supernatural train of Max Eyth's *Berufstragik*. My final claim, about the inevitable accommodation of scientific developments in myth, has, I hope, been demonstrated conclusively.

In order to have a meaningful debate about the third culture, we must understand its nineteenth-century roots. In an article entitled "Science and the Story That We Need," Neil Postman describes the nineteenth century as either a darkening or an enlightening historical moment, depending on one's point of view. It was an era in which many—seemingly almost all—of the age-old truths that had guided people since time immemorial were in flux. Postman emphasizes that the old explanatory narratives seemed inadequate in a world made paradoxically smaller by rail

11. Sternberger, *Panorama of the Nineteenth Century*, 27.

and other technologies, yet still larger than people could grasp.[12] The technicians recognized that they could not go back to simpler times and simpler tales. Many poets, philosophers, and social commentators also recognized this, and most of them lamented it. What they needed was the point of view articulated by such contemporaries as Berthold Auerbach (in "Ein Tag in der Heimat") and by twentieth-century third-culture thinkers like Adorno, Horkheimer, Sternberger, and Snow. They needed to find a way to retell the old tales so that they could encompass the new scientific and technological truths.

The task ahead for third-culture studies is to continue to look at how newer and newer innovations are accommodated in an ever-expanding narrative in the twenty-first century. The computer revolution has had as great an impact on our lives as the invention of the railway had on those of the nineteenth century. The speed of computer advances continually complicates and challenges our understanding of our world. And it is only one of the many technologies evolving all around us. We are limited by our own historical context and perspective, and we, like those who came before us, tend to see contemporary technologies as the final discourse, the last narrative. And we still often make the mistake of thinking that the current technologies will sound the death knell of mythology. But history suggests that this is just another myth, and that as it was before, so will it always be: new technologies will continue to supersede the old, complicating our picture of the world and challenging us to expand the older narratives or to find new narratives for explaining ourselves and our world.

12. Neil Postman, "Science and the Story That We Need," *First Things* 69 (1997): 29–32.

APPENDIX A: "IM NACHTZUG"

FROM GERHART HAUPTMANN, *SAEMTLICHE WERKE*

© Propylaeen Verlag in der Ullstein Buchverlage GmbH, Berlin.
Reprinted by permission.

      Es poltert der Zug durch die Mondscheinnacht,
      Die Räder dröhnen und rasen.
      Still sitz' ich im Polster und halte die Wacht
      unter sieben schnarchenden Nasen.
05   Die Lampe flackert und zittert und zuckt,
      und der Wagen rasselt und rüttelt und ruckt,
      und weit, wie ins Reich der Gespenster,
      weit blick' ich hinaus in das dämmrige Licht,
      und schemenhaft schau' ich mein blasses Gesicht
10   im lampenbeschienenen Fenster.

      Da rast es nun hin mit dem brausenden Zug
      an Wiesen und Wäldern vorüber,
      über Mauern, Stakete und Bäume im Flug,
      und trüber blickt es und trüber.
15   Und jetzo, wahrhaftig, ich täusche mich nicht,
      jetzt rollen über mein Schattengesicht
      zwei schwere und leuchtende Tränen.
      Und tief in der Brust mir klingt es und singt's,
      Und fiebernd das Herz und die Pulse durchdringt's,
20   ein wildes, ein brennendes Sehnen.

Ein Sehnen hinaus in das Mondscheinreich,
das fliegend die Drähte durchschneiden.
Sie tauchen hernieder und steigen zugleich,
Vom Zauber der Nacht mich zu scheiden.
Doch ich blicke hinaus, und das Herz wird mir weit,
und ich lulle mich ein in die selige Zeit,
wo nächtlich tanzte am Weiher
auf Mondlichtstrahlen die Elfenmaid,
dazu ihr von minniger Wonne und Leid
der Elfe spielte die Leier.

Der Elfe, er spielte die Leier so schön,
die Gräslein mußten ihm lauschen,
der Mühlbach im Sturze vernahm's und blieb stehn,
vergessend sein eigenes Rauschen.
Maiblume und Rotklee weineten Tau,
und wonnige Schauer durchbebten die Au,
und Sänger lauschten im Haine.
Sie lauschten und lernten vom Elfen gar viel
und stimmten ihr duftendes Saitenspiel
so zaubrisch und rein wie das seine.

Vorüber, vorüber im sausenden Takt!
Kein Zauber nimmt dich gefangen,
der du schwindelhoch über dem Katarakt
und tief durch die Berge gegangen.
Du rasender Pulsschlag der fiebernden Welt,
du Dämon, der in den Armen mich hält
und trägt zu entlegener Ferne!
Ich bliebe so gerne im Mondenschein
und lauschte so gerne verschwiegen allein
der Zwiesprach' seliger Sterne!

Rauchwolken verhüllen das dämmernde Bild
und schlingen weißwogende Reigen.
Doch unter mir stampft es und schmettert es wild,
und unter mir will es nicht schweigen.

55 Es klingt wie ein Ächzen, es rieselt wie Schweiß,
als schleppten Zyklopen hin über das Gleis
den Zug auf ehernen Armen.
Und wie ich noch lausche, beklommen und bang,
da wird aus dem Chaos ein Donnergesang,
60 zum Grauen zugleich und Erbarmen:

"Wir tragen euch hin durch die duftende Nacht,
mit keuchenden Kehlen und Brüsten.
Wir haben euch güldene Häuser gemacht,
Indessen wie Geier wir nisten.
65 Wir schaffen euch Kleider. Wir backen euch Brot.
Ihr schafft uns den grinsenden, winselnden Tod.
Wir wollen die Ketten zerbrechen.
Uns dürstet, uns dürstet nach eurem Gut!
Uns dürstet, uns dürstet nach eurem Blut!
70 Wir wollen uns rächen, uns rächen!

Wohl sind wir ein rauhes, blutdürstend Geschlecht,
mit schwieligen Händen und Herzen.
Doch gibt uns zum Leben, zum Streben ein Recht
und nehmt uns die Last unserer Schmerzen!
75 Ja, könnten wir atmen, im keuchenden Lauf,
nur einmal erquickend, tief innerlich auf,
so, weil du den Elfen bewundert,
so sängen wir dir mit Donnergetön
das Lied, so finster und doch so schön,
80 das Lied von unserem Jahrhundert!"

Willst lernen, Poetlein, das heilige Lied,
so lausche dem Rasseln der Schienen,
so meide das schläfrige, tändelnde Ried
und folge dem Gang der Maschinen;
85 beachte den Funken im singenden Draht,
des Schiffes schwindelnden Wolkenpfad,
und weiter, o beuge dich nieder
zum Herzen der Armen, mitleidig und mild,
und was es dir zitternd und weinend enthüllt,
90 ersteh' es in Tönen dir wieder!

Es poltert der Zug durch die Mondscheinnacht,
die Räder dröhnen und rasen.
Still sitz' ich im Polster und halte die Wacht
unter sieben schnarchenden Nasen.
95   Die Lampe flackert und zittert und zuckt,
und der Wagen rasselt und rüttelt und ruckt,
und tief aus dem Chaos der Töne,
da quillt es, da drängt es, da perlt es empor
wie Hymnengesänge, bezaubernd mein Ohr,
100 in erdenverklärender Schöne.

Und leise auf schwillt es, und ebbend verhallt's
im schmetternden Eisengeklirre.
Und wieder erwacht es, und himmelauf wallt's
Hervor aus dem Tönegewirre.
105 Und immer von neuem versinkt es und steigt.
Und endlich verweht's im Tumulte und schweigt
und läßt mir ein heißes Begehren,
das sinneberückende Zaubergetön
von himmlischen Lenzen auf irdischen Höhn
110 zu Ende, zu Ende zu hören.

APPENDIX B: "DIE BRÜCK' AM TAY"

When shall we three meet again?
    Macbeth

"Wann treffen wir drei wieder zusammen?"
"Um die siebente Stund', am Brückendamm"
    "Am Mittelpfeiler."
                "Ich lösche die Flamm."
05 "Ich mit."

    "Ich komme vom Norden her."
    "Und ich vom Süden."
                "Und ich vom Meer."

    "Hei, das gibt einen Ringelreihn,
10 Und die Brücke muß in den Grund hinein."

    "Und der Zug, der in die Brücke tritt
    Um die siebente Stund'?"
                "Ei, der muß mit."
    "Muß mit."

15   "Tand, Tand,
    Ist das Gebilde von Menschenhand!"

Auf der *Norder*seite, das Brückenhaus -
Alle Fenster sehen nach Süden aus,
Und die Brückersleut' ohne Rast und Ruh
20 Und in Bangen sehen nach Süden zu,
Sehen und warten, ob nicht ein Licht
Übers Wasser hin "Ich komme" spricht,
"Ich komme, trotz Nacht und Sturmesflug,
Ich, der Edinburger Zug."

25 Und der Brückner jetzt: "Ich seh' einen Schein
Am anderen Ufer. Das muß er sein.
Nun, Mutter, weg mit dem bangen Traum,
Unser Johnie kommt und will seinen Baum,
Und was noch am Baume von Lichtern ist,
30 Zünd' alles an wie zum heiligen Christ,
Der will heuer *zweimal* mit uns sein, -
Und in elf Minuten ist er herein."

Und es war der Zug. Am *Süder*thurm
Keucht er vorbei jetzt gegen Sturm,
35 Und Johnie spricht: "Die Brücke noch!
Aber was thut es, wir zwingen es doch.
Ein fester Kessel, ein doppelter Dampf,
Die bleiben Sieger in solchem Kampf.
Und wie's auch rast und ringt und rennt,
40 Wir kriegen es unter: das Element.

Und unser Stolz ist unsre Brück';
Ich lache, denk' ich an früher zurück,
An all den Jammer und all die Noth
Mit dem elend alten Schifferboot;
45 Wie manche liebe Christfestnacht
Hab ich im Fährhaus zugebracht
Und sah unsrer Fenster lichten Schein
Und zählte, und konnte nicht drüben sein."

50 Auf der Norderseite, das Brückenhaus -
Alle Fenster sehen nach Süden aus,

Und die Brücknersleut' ohne Rast und Ruh
Und in Bangen sehen nach Süden zu;
Denn wüthender wurde der Winde Spiel,
Und jetzt, als ob Feuer vom Himmel fiel',
Erglüht es in niederschießender Pracht
Überm Wasser unten...Und wieder ist Nacht.

"Wann treffen wir drei wieder zusammen?"
"Um Mitternacht, am Bergeskamm,"
"Auf dem hohen Moor, am Erlenstamm."

"Ich komme."
    "Ich mit."
        "Ich nenn' euch die Zahl."
"Und ich die Namen."
        "Und ich die Qual."
"Hei!"
    "Wie Splitter brach es entzwei."

        "Tand, Tand,
Ist das Gebilde von Menschenhand."

BIBLIOGRAPHY

Primary Sources

Auerbach, Berthold. *Sträflinge* (1846). In *Gesammelte Schriften,* 3:1–100. Stuttgart: J. G. Cottasche, 1857–58.

———. "Auf einem Acker an der Eisenbahn" (1845). In *Gesammelte Schriften,* 17:214–17. Stuttgart: J. G. Cottasche, 1857–58.

———. *Das Nest an der Bahn* (1876). In *Auerbachs Sämtliche Schwarzwälder Dorfgeschichten,* 10:1–126. Stuttgart: J. G. Cottasche, n.d.

———. "Ein Tag in der Heimat." *Deutsche Rundschau* 23 (1880): 289–303.

Bäumer, Gertrud. "Dichtung und Maschinenzeitalter." *Die Frau* 14 (1907): 267–75.

Bölsche, Wilhelm. *Die naturwissenschaftlichen Grundlagen der Poesie.* 1887; Tübingen: Max Niemeyer, 1976.

Eucken, Rudolf. "Der innere Mensch am Ausgang des 19. Jahrhunderts." *Deutsche Rundschau* 92 (1897): 29–48.

Eyth, Max. *Berufstragik* (1899). In *Hinter Pflug und Schraubstock: Skizzen aus dem Taschenbuch eines Ingenieurs,* 415–557. Stuttgart: Deutsche Verlags Anstalt, n.d.

———. "Foreword." In *Lebendige Kräfte: Sieben Vorträge aus dem Gebiete der Technik.* Berlin: Springer, 1905.

———. "Poesie und Technik." In *Lebendige Kräfte: Sieben Vorträge aus dem Gebiete der Technik,* 1–24. Berlin: Springer, 1905.

Fontane, Theodor. "Unsere epische und lyrische Poesie seit 1848" (1853). In *Aufsätze, Kritiken, Erinnerungen,* ed. Jürgen Kolbe. Sec. 3, vol. 1 of *Sämtliche Werke,* ed. Walter Keitel, 236–60. Munich: Hanser, 1969.

———. "Die Brück' am Tay" (1880). In *Romane, Erzählungen, Gedichte.* Sec. 1, vol. 6 of *Sämtliche Werke,* ed. Walter Keitel, 285–87. Munich: Hanser, 1964.

———. "Der Zug nach dem Westen" (review, 1886). In *Aufsätze, Kritiken, Erinnerungen,* ed. Jürgen Kolbe. Sec. 3, vol. 1 of *Sämtliche Werke,* ed. Walter Keitel, 561–70. Munich: Hanser, 1969.

———. *Cécile* (1887). In *Romane, Erzählungen, Gedichte.* Sec. 1, vol. 2 of *Sämtliche Werke,* ed. Walter Keitel, 141–317. Munich: Hanser, 1962.

———. *Effi Briest* (1895). In *Romane, Erzählungen, Gedichte*. Sec. 1, vol. 4 of *Sämtliche Werke*, ed. Walter Keitel, 7–296. Munich: Hanser, 1963.

———. *In Freiheit dienen: Briefe von Theodor Fontane*, ed. Friedrich Seebaß. Munich: Hanser, 1956.

Freud, Sigmund. *The Future of an Illusion*. In *The Freud Reader*, ed. Peter Gay, 685–722. 1927; New York: W. W. Norton, 1995.

———. *Civilization and Its Discontents*. In *The Freud Reader*, ed. Peter Gay, 722–72. 1930; New York: W. W. Norton, 1995.

Hauptmann, Gerhart. *Bahnwärter Thiel* (1888). In *Sämtliche Werke*, comp. Hans-Egon Hass, 6:35–67. Berlin: Propyläen, 1963.

———. "Im Nachtzug" (1888). In *Ausgewählte Werke*, comp. Josef Gregor, 5:12–14. Gütersloh: C. Bertelsmann Verlag, 1954.

———. *Das Abenteuer meiner Jugend* (1932). In *Sämtliche Werke*, comp. Hans-Egon Hass, 7:451–1082. Berlin: Propyläen, 1962.

Heine, Heinrich. "Letter of 5 May 1843." In *Sämtliche Werke*, ed. Volkmar Hansen, 14:56–64. Hamburg: Hoffmann und Campe, 1990.

List, Friedrich. *Kräfte und Mächte*. 1841; Munich: Langewiesche-Brandt, 1942.

Nietzsche, Friedrich. "Genealogy of Morals." In *Basic Writings of Nietzsche*, trans. and ed. Walter Kaufmann, 449–599. 1887; New York: Modern Library, 2000.

Rosegger, Peter. "Der Dorfbahnhof" (1868). In *Alpensommer*, 262–69. Leipzig: L. Staackmann, 1938.

———. *Die neue Bahn* (1873). Berlin: Deutsche Landbuchhandlung, 1924.

———. "Bei Berthold Auerbach, eine Erinnerung von P. K. Rosegger." *Heimgarten* 6 (1882): 441–45.

———. "Dem Andenken Berthold Auerbachs." *Heimgarten* 15 (1891): 275–81.

———. "Die neue Hochschwabbahn." *Heimgarten* 18 (1894): 628–31.

———. *Das ewige Licht* (1895). Munich: L. Staackmann, n.d.

———. "Religiöse Bedeutung der Wissenschaft." *Heimgarten* 20 (1895): 148–50.

———. "Alte und neue Schönheit." *Heimgarten* 20 (1896): 442.

———. "Das Dampfroß mein Pegasus." *Heimgarten* 20 (1896): 448–51.

———. "Am 24. Mai." *Heimgarten* 30 (1906): 788.

Schmidt, Julian. "Die Verwirrung der Romantik und die Dorfgeschichte Auerbachs." In *Theorie des bürgerlichen Realismus*, ed. Gerhard Plumpe, 106–10. 1860; Stuttgart: Philip Reclam, 1985.

Secondary Sources

Adorno, Theodor, and Max Horkheimer. *Dialectic of Enlightenment*. 1944; New York: Continuum, 1989.

Bibliography 165

Alderman, Harold. "Technology as Phenomenon." *The Personalist* 51 (1970): 535–45.
Aust, Hugo. *Theodor Fontane: "Verklärung."* In *Eine Untersuchung zum Ideengehalt seiner Werke.* Bonn: Bouvier, 1974.
Bance, Alan. *Theodor Fontane: The Major Novels.* Cambridge: Cambridge University Press, 1982.
———. "Fontane and the Notion of Progress." *Publications of the English Goethe Society* 57 (1988): 1–18.
Bell, Robert F. "'Und alle fahren mit': The Train as Symbol and Setting in German Literature from Hauptmann to Borchert." *Studies in Nineteenth Century German Literature* 3 (1974): 1–11.
Bernd, Clifford Albrecht. *German Poetic Realism.* Boston: Twayne 1981.
Bowen, Zack, and David L. Wilson. *Science and Literature: Bridging the Two Cultures.* Gainesville: University Press of Florida, 2001.
Brinkmann, Richard. *Theodor Fontane: Über die Verbindlichkeit des Unverbindlichen.* Munich: Piper, 1967.
Brockmann, John, ed. *The Third Culture.* New York: Simon and Schuster, 1995.
Brophy, James M. *Capitalism, Politics, and Railroads in Prussia, 1830–1870.* Columbus: Ohio State University Press, 1998.
Brown, Raymond E. *An Introduction to the New Testament.* New York: Doubleday, 1997.
Carr, Gilbert. "Entgleisung und Dekonstruktion: Theodor Fontane's *Die Brück' am Tay.*" In *Das schwierige neunzehnte Jahrhundert,* ed. Jürgen Barkhoff, 319–33. Tubingen: Niemeyer, 2000.
Chambers, Helen Elizabeth. *Supernatural and Irrational Elements in the Works of Theodor Fontane.* Stuttgart: Heinz, 1980.
———. *The Changing Image of Theodor Fontane.* Columbia, S.C.: Camden House, 1997.
Clouser, Robin A. "The Spiritual Malaise of a Modern Hercules, Hauptmann's *Bahnwärter Thiel.*" *Germanic Review* 50 (1980): 98–108.
Demetz, Peter. *Formen des Realismus: Theodor Fontane, Kritische Untersuchungen.* Munich: Hanser, 1964.
Dow, James R., and James P. Sandrock. "Peter Rosegger's *Erdsegen:* The Function of Folklore in the Work of an Austrian *Heimatdichter.*" *Journal of the Folklore Institute* 19 (1976): 227–39.
Downing, Eric. *Double Exposures: Repetition and Realism in Nineteenth-Century German Fiction.* Stanford: Stanford University Press, 2000.
Fremdling, Rainer. "Industrialisierung und Eisenbahn." In *Zug der Zeit—Zeit der Züge: Deutsche Eisenbahn, 1835–1985,* vol. 1, ed. Manfred Jehle and Franz Sonnenberger. Berlin: Siedler, 1985.
Frischler, Kurt. *Das grosse Österreichische Eisenbahnbuch.* Vienna: Fritz Molden, 1979.

Furst, Lillian. *All Is True: The Claims and Strategies of Realist Fiction.* Durham: Duke University Press, 1995.
Grant, Michael, and John Hazel. *Who's Who in Classical Mythology.* Oxford: Oxford University Press, 1993.
Green, Abigail. *Fatherlands: State-Building and Nationhood in Nineteenth-Century Germany.* Cambridge: Cambridge University Press, 2001.
Das große Conversations-Lexicon für gebildete Stände, vol. 8. Hildburghausen: J. Meyer, 1846.
Guidry, Glen A. "Myth and Ritual in Fontane's *Effi Briest.*" *Germanic Review* 59, no. 1 (1984): 19–25.
Haslinger, Franz. "Ein Herold Adalbert Stifters: Roseggers fünfzigjähriges Wirken für die Anerkennung von Stifters Gesamtwerk." *Oberösterreichische Heimatblätter* 2 (1948): 320.
Heinimann, Alfred Ch. *Technische Innovation und literarische Aneignung: Die Eisenbahn in der deutschen und englischen Literatur des 19. Jahrhunderts.* Bern: Francke, 1992.
Herman, Luc. "Die Nachwirkung der Idyllentradition bei der Rezeption der Dorfgeschichte im programmatischen Realismus." *Etudes Germaniques* 42 (1987): 16–28.
Heuss, Theodor. *Deutsche Gestalten: Studien zum 19. Jahrhundert.* Stuttgart: Wunderlich, 1951.
Hewitt, Paul G. *Conceptual Physics.* Menlo Park, Calif.: Addison-Wesley, 1997.
Holub, Robert C. *Reflections of Realism: Paradox, Norm, and Ideology in Nineteenth-Century German Prose.* Detroit: Wayne State University Press, 1991.
Horch, Hans Otto. "Berthold Auerbach's First Collection of *Dorfgeschichten* Appears." In *Yale Companion to Jewish Writing and Thought in German Culture, 1096–1996,* ed. Sander L. Gilman and Jack Zipes, 158–63. New Haven: Yale University Press, 1997.
Jehle, Manfred, and Franz Sonnenberger, eds. *Zug der Zeit—Zeit der Züge: Deutsche Eisenbahn, 1835–1985.* 2 vols. Berlin: Siedler, 1985.
Johnstone, Barbara, ed. *Repetition in Discourse: Interdisciplinary Perspectives.* Norwood, N.J.: Ablex, 1994.
Jolles, Charlotte. *Theodor Fontane.* Stuttgart: Metzler, 1993.
Korte, Hermann. *Ordnung und Tabu: Studien zum poetischen Realismus.* Bonn: Bouvier, 1989.
Lepenies, Wolf. "The Direction of the Disciplines: The Future of the Universities." *Comparative Criticism* 11 (1989): 51–70.
Mahr, Johannes. *Eisenbahnen in der deutschen Dichtung: Der Wandel eines literarischen Motivs im 19. und im beginnenden 20. Jahrhundert.* Munich: Fink, 1982.
Martini, Fritz. *Das Wagnis der Sprache: Interpretationen deutscher Prosa von Nietzsche bis Benn.* Stuttgart: Ernst Klett, 1956.
———. "Theodor Fontane, 'Die Brück' am Tay.'" In *Wege zum Gedicht: Inter-*

pretationen von Balladen, ed. Rupert Hirschenauer and Albrecht Weber, 377–92. Munich: Schnell and Steiner, 1963.

Maurer, Warren R. *Gerhart Hauptmann.* Boston: Twayne, 1982.

———. *Understanding Gerhart Hauptmann.* Columbia: University of South Carolina Press, 1992.

McInnes, Edward. "Auerbach's *Schwarzwälder Dorfgeschichten* and the Quest for German Realism in the 1840's." In *Perspectives on German Realist Writing: Eight Essays,* ed. Mark G. Ward, 93–111. Lewiston, N.Y.: Mellen, 1995.

Mierzejewski, Alfred C. *The Most Valuable Asset of the Reich: A History of the German National Railway,* vol. 1. Chapel Hill: University of North Carolina Press, 1999.

Möser, Kurt. "Max Eyths Technikthematisierung im Kontext der Technikdebatte." *Anstösse* 32 (1985): 102–13.

Müller-Seidel, Walter. *Theodor Fontane: Soziale Romankunst in Deutschland.* Stuttgart: Metzler, 1975.

Post, Klaus D. "Afterword" to *Bahnwärter Thiel,* by Gerhart Hauptmann, 44–146. Munich: Hanser, 1979.

Postman, Neil. "Science and the Story That We Need." *First Things* 69 (1997): 29–32.

Rademacher, Gerhard. *Technik und industrielle Arbeitswelt in der deutschen Lyrik des 19. und 20. Jahrhunderts: Versuch einer Bestandsaufnahme.* Frankfurt: Peter Lang, 1976.

Reuter, Hans-Heinrich. *Fontane.* 2 vols. Berlin: Verlag der Nation, 1995.

Schivelbusch, Wolfgang. *The Railway Journey: The Industrialization of Time and Space in the Nineteenth Century.* Hamburg: Berg, 1977.

Schöpfer, Gerald. "Peter Rosegger: Ein glaubwürdiger Zeuge wirtschafts- und sozialgeschichtlicher Veränderungen." In *Fremd gemacht? Der Volksschriftsteller Peter Rosegger,* ed. Uwe Baur, 25–42. Vienna: Böhlau, 1988.

Schwann, Mathieu. *Ludwig Camphausen.* Essen, 1915.

Segeberg, Harro. *Literarische Technik-Bilder: Studien zum Verhältnis von Technik- und Literaturgeschichte im 19. und frühen 20. Jahrhundert.* Tübingen: Niemeyer, 1987.

———. *Literatur im technischen Zeitalter: Von der Frühzeit der Deutschen Aufklärung bis zum Beginn des Ersten Weltkriegs.* Darmstadt: Wissenschaftliche Buchgesellschaft, 1997.

Shaffer, Elinor S., ed. *The Third Culture: Literature and Science.* Berlin: De Gruyter, 1998.

Silz, Walter. *Realism and Reality: Studies in the German Novella of Poetic Realism.* Chapel Hill: University of North Carolina Press, 1962.

Snow, C. P. "The Two Cultures" (1959), in C. P. Snow, *The Two Cultures,* 1–51. Cambridge: Cambridge University Press, 1993.

———. "The Two Cultures: A Second Look" (1963), in C. P. Snow, *The Two Cultures,* 53–100. Cambridge: Cambridge University Press, 1993.

168   Bibliography

Stern, J. P. "*Effi Briest, Madame Bovary, Anna Karenina.*" *Modern Language Review* 52 (1957): 363–75.

Sternberger, Dolf. *Panorama of the Nineteenth Century.* 1938; New York: Urizen, 1977.

Stroud, Dean Garrett. "Idyll as Possibility: Rosegger's Humanism." *Modern Austrian Literature* 21, no. 2 (1988): 23–40.

Subiotto, Frances M. "The Ghost in *Effi Briest.*" *Forum for Modern Language Studies* 21, no. 2 (1985): 137–50.

Swales, Erika. "Private Mythologies and Public Unease: On Fontane's *Effi Briest.*" *Modern Language Review* 75 (1980): 114–24.

Völkel, Markus. "Einigkeit und Freiheit: Die Eisenbahn, ein Mittel nationaler Politik." In *Zug der Zeit—Zeit der Züge: Deutsche Eisenbahn, 1835–1985,* vol. 1, ed. Manfred Jehle and Franz Sonnenberger. Berlin: Siedler, 1985.

Wagner, Karl. *Die literarische Öffentlichkeit der Provinzliteratur: Der Volksschriftsteller Peter Rosegger.* Tübingen: Niemeyer, 1991.

Watson, Peter. *The Modern Mind: An Intellectual History of the Twentieth Century.* New York: Harper-Collins, 2001.

Williams, D. A. *The Monster in the Mirror: Studies in Nineteenth-Century Realism.* Oxford: Oxford University Press, 1980.

Wilson, Edward O. *Consilience: The Unity of Knowledge.* New York: Knopf, 1998.

INDEX

Das Abenteuer meiner Jugend (The Adventure of My Youth). See Hauptmann, Gerhart
"Auf einem Acker an der Eisenbahn" (On a Field Next to the Railway). *See* Auerbach, Berthold
Adorno, Theodor, ix–x, 2, 20–23, 35, 37, 54, 61, 65, 72, 80, 88, 97, 108 154; *Dialectic of Enlightenment,* 20–23
Auerbach, Berthold, ix, 1, 2, 8, 10, 12, 14, 15, 21, 22, 23, 24, 27–54, 55, 56, 57–60, 61, 62, 63, 64, 65, 66, 76, 80, 85, 87, 96, 98, 108, 112, 130, 131, 154; "Auf einem Acker an der Eisenbahn" (On a Field Next to the Railway), 24, 29–31, 65; on antisemitism, 8–9; critique of Romanticism, 36; *Das Nest an der Bahn (The Nest on the Railway),* 14, 21, 23, 24, 29, 33, 38, 44, 45–54, 65; realism, 28, 31–39, 43–44, 47, 50; *Schwarzwälder Dorfgeschichten (Black Forest Village Tales),* 1, 24, 30, 31, 32, 58; *Sträflinge (Convicts),* 1, 23, 24, 28, 33, 38, 39–44, 45, 47, 53, 54, 77, 98; "Ein Tag in der Heimat" (One Day in My Homeland), 8, 10, 12, 21, 24, 27, 28, 34–38, 40, 43, 59, 61, 87, 130, 131, 154; *versöhnung* (reconciliation), 37–38, 53
Aust, Hugo, 86

Bahnwärter Thiel (The Linesman Thiel). See Hauptmann, Gerhart
Bance, Alan, 107–8

Bäumer, Gertrud, 32, 33, 41
Berufstragik (Occupational Tragedy). See Eyth, Max
Der blonde Eckbert (Eckbert the Fair). See Tieck, Ludwig
Bölsche, Wilhelm, 17–18, 19, 20, 21, 26, 35, 37, 38, 54, 60, 61, 130–31, 132, 133, 150; *Die Naturwissenschaftlichen Grundlagen der Poesie (The Scientific Bases of Poetry),* 17–18, 132
Bowen, Zack, 150; *Science and Literature: Bridging the Two Cultures,* 150
Brinkmann, Richard, 102
Brockman, John, 151; *The Third Culture,* 151
"Die Brück' am Tay" (The Bridge over the Tay). *See* Fontane, Theodor

Camphausen, Ludwig, 16–17, 18, 19, 21, 54, 60, 110, 120, 138
Cécile. See Fontane, Theodor
Chambers, Helen Elizabeth, 88, 93, 95, 96–97, 102, 103, 104, 135–36
Civilization and Its Discontents. See Freud, Sigmund
Clouser, Robin A., 124, 125, 126–27
Consilience: The Unity of Knowledge. See Wilson, Edward O.

"Das Dampfroß mein Pegasus" (The Steamhorse my Pegasus). *See* Rosegger, Peter
Decameron, 123

169

Index

Deutsche Rundschau, 8
Dialectic of Enlightenment. See Adorno, Theodor; Horkheimer, Max
"Der Dorfbahnhof" (The Village Train Station). *See* Rosegger, Peter
Downing, Eric, 18, 37, 47, 60, 88, 94

Effi Briest. See Fontane, Theodor
Eisenbahnen in der deutschen Dichtung. Der Wandel eines literarischen Motivs im 19. und im beginnenden 20. Jahrhundert (Railways in German Poetry: The Transformation of a Literary Motif in the Nineteenth and Early Twentieth Century). See Johannes Mahr
enlightenment: *Dialectic of Enlightenment*, 2, 20–23; and myth, ix-x, 20–23, 42, 44, 61, 63, 65, 68, 72, 88, 91, 92, 94, 95–96, 97, 100, 104, 108, 138
"Erlkönig" (The Erl-King). See Goethe, Johann Wolfgang von
Eucken, Rudolf, 19, 110, 132, 138, 150
Das ewige Licht (Eternal Light). See Rosegger, Peter
Eyth, Max, 1, 2, 15, 24, 26, 128–48, 153; *Berufstragik (Occupational Tragedy)*, 1, 26, 129, 134, 138–48, 153; *Lebendige Kräfte (Living Forces)*, 26, 130; "Poesie und Technik" (Poetry and Technology), 26, 128, 130–34, 144, 146, 148; realism, 132–33, 142; on Rosegger, 131, 132

Firth of Tay, collapse, 129, 134–35, 141, 143
Fontane, Theodor, ix, 2, 15, 16, 23, 24, 25, 26, 37, 38, 58, 84–108, 113, 128, 129, 134–38, 139, 140, 145, 146, 147; "Die Brück' am Tay" (The Bridge over the Tay), 15, 26, 86, 129–30, 134–38, 146, 147, 159–61; *Cécile*, 23, 25, 85, 86, 88, 89–100, 101, 102, 105, 138, 143; *Effi Briest*, 16, 23, 25, 85, 86, 88, 100–108, 138; "Meine Gräber" (My Graves), 15; realism, 86–88; *Vor dem Sturm (Before the Storm)*, 84; "Unsere lyrische und epische Poesie seit 1848" (Our Lyric and Epic Poetry since 1848), 25, 37, 86–88; *verklärung* transfiguration, 37, 86, 87; *Der Zug nach dem Westen (The Train West)*, review of, 25, 87
Fowler, John, 129
Freud, Sigmund, 8, 11, 12, 19, 20; *Civilization and Its Discontents*, 8, 11; *The Future of an Illusion*, 19–20
Frischler, Kurt, 57
Furst, Lilian, 4, 18, 37, 60, 66, 141
The Future of an Illusion. See Freud, Sigmund

German Agricultural Society, 129
Gerstner, Franz Anton Ritter von, 56–57
Glaser, Adolph, 89
Goethe, Johann Wolfgang von, 116, 120; "Erlkönig" (The Erl-King), 116, 120; *unerhörte Begebenheit* (unheard-of-occurrence), 123
Grant, Michael, 117
Green, Abigail, 7–9
Die Grenzboten, 32

Hauptmann, Gerhart, ix, 2, 24, 25, 70, 81, 108, 109–27, 136; *Das Abenteuer meiner Jugend (The Adventure of My Youth)*, 111–12; *Bahnwärter Thiel (The Linesman Thiel)*, 24, 25, 26, 70, 81, 109, 110, 111, 112, 113, 114, 121–27, 143, 145, 147; myth, 112–14, 115–20, 124; "Im Nachtzug" (In the Night Train), 24, 25, 112, 114, 115–20, 125, 127, 136, 156–58; realism, 112–14; *Die Weber (The Weavers)*, 112
Hazel, John, 117
Heimgarten. See Rosegger, Peter
Heine, Heinrich, 11–12, 15, 29, 81, 84
Heinimann, Alfred Ch., 5, 40, 45, 47,

Index   171

68, 85, 91–92, 96, 101, 104, 106, 107, 122–23, 136, 137, 139, 143; *Technische Innovation und literarische Aneignung: Die Eisenbahn in der deutschen und englischen Literatur des 19. Jahrhunderts* (*Technical Innovation and Literary Appropriation: The Railway in German and British Literature of the Nineteenth Century*), 13–14, 15
Helmholtz, Hermann von, 28
Hermann, Luc, 33
Hoffmann, E. T. A., 120; *Der Sandmann* (*The Sandman*), 120
Holub, Robert C., 26, 37, 113
Holz, Arno, 123; *Papa Hamlet*, 123
Horkheimer, Max, ix–x, 2, 20–23, 35, 37, 54, 61, 65, 72, 80, 88, 97, 108, 154; *Dialectic of Enlightenment*, 20–23

Johnstone, Barbara, 47, 50, 76, 90–91

Kräfte und Mächte (*Forces and Powers*). *See* List, Friedrich
Kretzer, Max, 87, 113; *Meister Timpe* (*Master Timpe*), 113

Lebendige Kräfte (*Living Forces*). *See* Eyth, Max
Lepenies, Wolf, 152
Lindau, Paul, 25, 87
List, Friedrich, 4–9, 30, 31, 41, 56, 81; *Kräfte und Mächte* (*Forces and Powers*), 4–5

Macbeth, 135–36, 159
Mahr, Johannes, 6, 12–14, 26, 43, 85–86, 114, 115–16, 119–20, 122–23, 126, 127, 134, 139, 150, 151–52; *Eisenbahnen in der deutschen Dichtung. Der Wandel eines literarischen Motivs im 19. und im beginnenden 20. Jahrhundert* (*Railways in German Poetry: The Transformation of a Literary Motif in the Nineteenth and Early Twentieth Century*), 12–14
Martini, Fritz, 122–23, 137–38

Maurer, Warren R., 114
McInnes, Edward, 31, 33, 41
"Meine Gräber" (My Graves). *See* Fontane, Theodor *Meister Timpe* (*Master Timpe*). *See* Krezer, Max
Metternich government, 57
Meyer's *Conversations-Lexicon*. *See* Railway System, Germany
The Modern Mind. *See* Watson, Peter
Möser, Kurt, 130
Müller-Seidel, Walter, 92, 99
myth: Bölsche, 17, 18; defined, 2, 19; and enlightenment, ix–x, 20–23, 42, 44, 61, 63, 65, 68, 72, 88, 91, 92, 94, 95–96, 97, 100, 104, 108, 138; Fontane, 85; Hauptmann, 112–14; Nietzsche, 1, 149; and science 17–18, 71, 83, 90–91, 108, 113, 117, 120, 130–34, 147, 152–54; and technology, ix–x, 2–3, 4, 17, 19, 20–23, 29, 30–31, 35, 43, 44, 50, 63, 64, 65, 69, 70, 72–73, 79–80, 82, 98, 102, 106, 117, 119, 126–27, 138, 140, 143, 144, 148, 151, 154

"Im Nachtzug" (In the Night Train). *See* Hauptmann, Gerhart
naturalism, 25, 45, 58, 86, 113
Die Naturwissenschaftlichen Grundlagen der Poesie (*The Scientific Bases of Poetry*). *See* Bölsche, Wilhelm
Nietzsche, Friedrich, 1, 149
Das Nest an der Bahn (*The Nest on the Railway*). *See* Auerbach, Berthold
Die neue Bahn (*The New Railway*). *See* Rosegger, Peter
"Die neue Hochschwabbahn" (The New Rail of the *Hochschwaben*). *See* Rosegger, Peter

Panorama of the Nineteenth Century. *See* Sternberger, Dolf
Papa Hamlet. *See* Holz, Arno; Schlaf, Johannes
"Poesie und Technik" (Poetry and Technology). *See* Eyth, Max
Post, Klaus, 109–11, 112, 113–14

Index

Postman, Neil, 153; "Science and the Story We Need", 153–54

Rademacher, Gerhard, 12, 14–15, 23, Rademacher, Gerhard, (cont) 24, 67, 153; *Technik und industrielle Arbeitswelt in der deutschen Lyrik des 19. und 20. Jahrhunderts* (*Technology and the Industrial Work Environment in the German Poetry of the Nineteenth and Twentieth Centuries*), 12
The Railway Journey. See Schivelbusch, Wolfgang
railway system, Austria, 56–57
railway system, Germany: described in Meyer's *Conversations-Lexicon*, 10–11; as economic engine, 5–6; history, 4–9, 31, 84, 109 (*see also* List, Friedrich); metaphors, 10, 30, 43–44; and realism 16–23; role in unification, 7–8; role in war, 5, 8, 19, 45–46, 47, 48; schematic representation in literature, 14–15
realism: and the railway, 16–23; relationship to science and technology, 3–4 (*see also* Rosegger), Peter; super realism, 26, 113; *See also* Auerbach, Berthold; Eyth, Max; Fontane, Theodor; Furst, Lilian; Hauptmann, Gerhart
"Religiöse Bedeutung der Wissenschaft" (The Religious Meaning of Science). *See* Rosegger, Peter
Reuter, Hans-Heinrich, 99
Rosegger, Peter, 2, 23, 24, 25, 38, 54, 55–83, 85, 87, 93, 96, 98, 108, 112, 116, 131, 132, 153; anti-semitism, 78; on Auerbach, 38; "Das Dampfroß mein Pegasus" (The Steamhorse my Pegasus), 25, 61–63; "Der Dorfbahnhof" (The Village Train Station), 25, 64–67, 80; *Das ewige Licht* (*Eternal Light*), 23, 25, 59, 73–83, 98, 112, 116; *Heimgarten*, 25, 58; *Die neue Bahn* (*The New Railway*), 23, 25, 67–73, 74, 82–83, 93, 98, 153; "Die neue Hochschwabbahn" (The New Rail of the *Hochschwaben*), 25, 63–64; Nobel prize, 57; on progress, 56, 58, 60–64; realism, 57–60, 66; "Religiöse Bedeutung der Wissenschaft" (The Religious Meaning of Science), 25, 60–61, 69, 72

Der Sandmann (*The Sandman*). *See* Hoffmann, E.T.A.
Schivelbusch, Wolfgang, 11, 15, 21, 23; *The Railway Journey*, 11, 15
Schlaf, Johannes, 123; *Papa Hamlet*, 123
Schmidt, Julian, 32, 33
Schöpfer, Gerald, 56
Schwarzwälder Dorfgeschichten (*Black Forest Village Tales*). *See* Auerbach, Berthold
science: and arts and humanities, x, 2, 15, 26, 130, 150–54; Bölsche, 17–18; and enlightenment 20–23, 54; Freud, 19; and myth 17–18, 71, 83, 90–91, 108, 113, 119, 120, 130–34, 147, 152–54; Nietzsche, 1; and realism, 3–4; and religion, 17–18, 19–20, 25, 60–61
Science and Literature: Bridging the Two Cultures. *See* Bowen, Zack; Wilson, David L.
"Science and the Story We Need." *See* Postman, Neil
Segeberg, Harro, 85, 101, 105, 129, 134, 135, 139–40, 141, 144, 147
Shaffer, Elinor S., 149, 150
Snow, C. P., x, 3, 130, 131, 150–54; "The Two Cultures", x, 150; "The Two Cultures: A Second Look", x, 150
Stern, J. P., 102
Sternberger, Dolf, 22, 30, 31, 44, 64, 125, 133, 136, 138, 152–53, 154; *Panorama of the Nineteenth Century*, 22–23, 30, 43–44, 125
Stifter, Adalbert, 34; *Bunte Steine* (*Colored Stones*), 34
Sträflinge (*Convicts*). *See* Auerbach, Berthold
Stroud, Dean, 58

Index 173

Vor dem Sturm (Before the Storm). *See* Fontane, Theodor
Stuttgart, Polytechnic Institute of, 129
Swales, Erika, 102, 107
"Ein Tag in der Heimat" (One Day in My Homeland). *See* Auerbach, Berthold
Technik und industrielle Arbeitswelt in der deutschen Lyrik des 19. und 20. Jahrhunderts (Technology and the Industrial Work Environment in the German Poetry of the Nineteenth and Twentieth Centuries). *See* Rademacher, Gerhard
Technische Innovation und literarische Aneignung: Die Eisenbahn in der deutschen und englischen Literatur des 19. Jahrhunderts (Technical Innovation and Literary Appropriation: The Railway in German and British Literature of the Nineteenth Century). *See* Heinimann, Alfred Ch.
technology: Adorno and Horkheimer, 20–23; Freud, 8, 11, 12; and literature, 13, 15–16, 26, 28, 85; and myth, ix-x, 2–3, 4, 17, 19, 20–23, 29, 30–31, 35, 43, 44, 50, 63, 64, 65, 69, 70, 72–73, 79–80, 82, 98, 102, 106, 117, 119, 126–27, 138, 140, 143, 144, 148, 151, 154; and nature, 14, 22–23, 64, 125, 136–38, 146; and poetry, 130; and realism 3–4; Schivelbusch, 11; and superstition, 68–69
third culture, x, 3, 26, 29, 37, 54, 60, 131, 139, 149–54
The Third Culture. *See* Brockman, John
Tieck, Ludwig, 123; *Der blonde Eckbert (Eckbert the Fair)*, 123–24
"The Two Cultures". *See* Snow, C. P.
"The Two Cultures: A Second Look". *See* Snow, C. P.

Völkel, Markus, 7, 8

Watson, Peter, x, 2–4, 149, 150; *The Modern Mind*, 2–4
Die Weber (The Weavers). *See* Hauptmann, Gerhard
Widman, Josef, 102
Williams, D. A., 88
Wilson, David L., 150; *Science and Literature: Bridging the Two Cultures*, 150
Wilson, Edward O., 151; *Consilience: The Unity of Knowledge*, 151

Young Germany, 34, 86

Der Zug nach dem Westen (The Train West), review of. *See* Fontane, Theodor

Black Devil and Iron Angel: The Railway in Nineteenth-Century German Realism was designed and composed in Bembo by Kachergis Book Design of Pittsboro, North Carolina. It was printed on 60-pound Natures Natural and bound by Thomson-Shore, Inc., of Dexter, Michigan.